Tai Tam -> Quarry Bay hike
Hong Kong Park + teahouse
Lamma
Cheung Chau
Po Toi s
✓ Sha Tin for duck
✓ Ozone
Dim sum in Sheung Wan
Dragons Back
✓ Maclehose trail
Sai Kung
✓ Sen Ryo
✓ Sham Shui Po / Stanley St.
Train sushi
Little Bao
✓ Butler
✓ Mak's Noodle, Central
001
Mido Cafe
Steamer baskets, Sai Ying Pun - Tak Cheung Sum Kee Bamboo Steamer Co.
Lau Sam Kee, Sham Shui Po

gestalten

The MONOCLE
Travel Guide Series

4

Hong Kong

Din Tai Fung
Goose in Tuen Mun
Hot Pot
Tai Lung Fung (bar)
FCC for a drink
Star Ferry
Social Place
Spring Deer
Happy Paradise
Fish School
Sumi Yakitori
Chinese Library
New Punjab Club
Ronin
Chairman
Loaf On, Sai Kung

For more information, please visit *gestalten.com*

Bibliographic information published by the Deutsche Nationalbibliothek: The Deutsche Nationalbibliothek lists this publication in the Deutsche Nationalbibliografie; detailed bibliographic data are available online at *dnb.d-nb.de*

MIX
Paper from responsible sources
FSC® C011712

This book was printed on paper certified by the FSC®

Monocle editor in chief: *Tyler Brûlé*
Monocle editor: *Andrew Tuck*
Series editor: *Nelly Gocheva*
Guide editor: *Aisha Speirs*

Designed by *Monocle*
Proofreading by *Monocle*
Typeset in *Plantin & Helvetica*

Printed by *Offsetdruckerei Grammlich, Pliezhausen*

Made in Germany

Published by *Gestalten*, Berlin 2015
ISBN 978-3-89955-576-9

2nd printing, 2015

Welcome
— See beyond the skyscrapers

Hong Kong has been a city of many identities: a *community of fishing villages*, a *refuge for immigrants*, an *international port* and a *British colony*. Today it continues to question its personality as it finds its place as part of *modern China*. It's a city where *global flagships* sit next to *independent cafés*; where *steel towers* dwarf *old shop houses* that are home to multiple generations of a single family. One moment you will be walking along a busy street; the next you'll be on a remote and quiet mountain trail.

As it's one of Asia's most connected business hubs we assume that many of you reading this travel guide will already know a bit about Hong Kong. As such, we're not going to take you to the most established restaurants, bars and shops, nor suggest you take the train out to Hong Kong Disneyland (if you really feel like a theme-park trip, you might as well go to local success story Ocean Park). Instead we show you that between meetings you can easily reach a nearby *surfing beach*, see works by *top contemporary artists* or get lost in *characterful backstreets*.

We'll point you where to go if you're in the mood for *bao* or *burgers*. And where to stay if you want to get away from the centre of town. There are *runs* and *hikes* to refresh you after you get off your long flight, plus essays from Hong Kongers who have witnessed some of the city's drastic changes over the past decade.

There is much more to Hong Kong than its sea of skyscrapers. Read on to discover a different side to this complex and ever-changing city. — (M)

Contents
— Navigating the city

Use the key below to help navigate the guide section by section.

- H Hotels
- F Food and drink
- R Retail
- T Things we'd buy
- E Essays
- C Culture
- D Design and architecture
- S Sport and fitness
- W Walks

Map
The city at a glance

Caught somewhere between being defined as a city and a territory, Hong Kong's 1,100 sq km are divided into Hong Kong Island, Kowloon, the New Territories and over 200 outlying islands. Many of these are more akin to glorified rocky outcrops but larger islands such as Lantau and Lamma form an important part of city life.

While some people will only leave Hong Kong Island to go to the airport, there are plenty of reasons to cross Victoria Harbour. In Kowloon there are neighbourhoods that many residents consider to be a more authentic version of Hong Kong. And in the country parks and farms of the New Territories it's easy to forget that you're in a city at all.

From the old colonial houses on the Peak and the steel towers of Central (which often pierce the clouds) to Kowloon's industrial neighbourhoods and Sai Kung's tranquil beaches, Hong Kong is much more than just a concrete jungle.

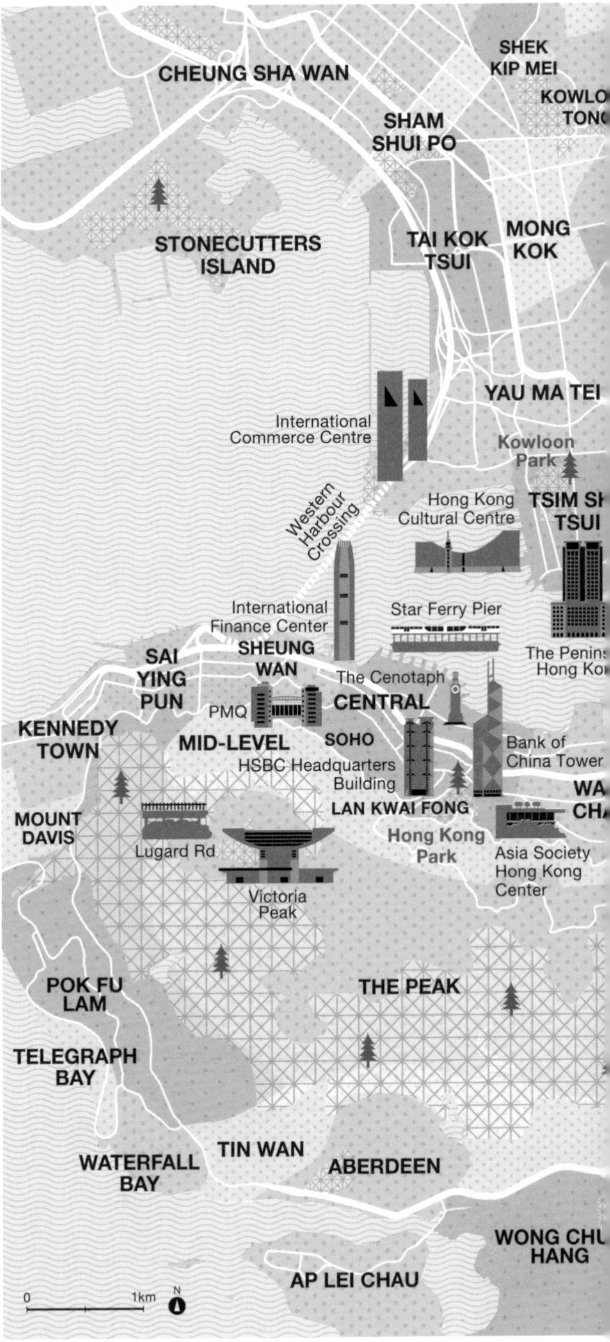

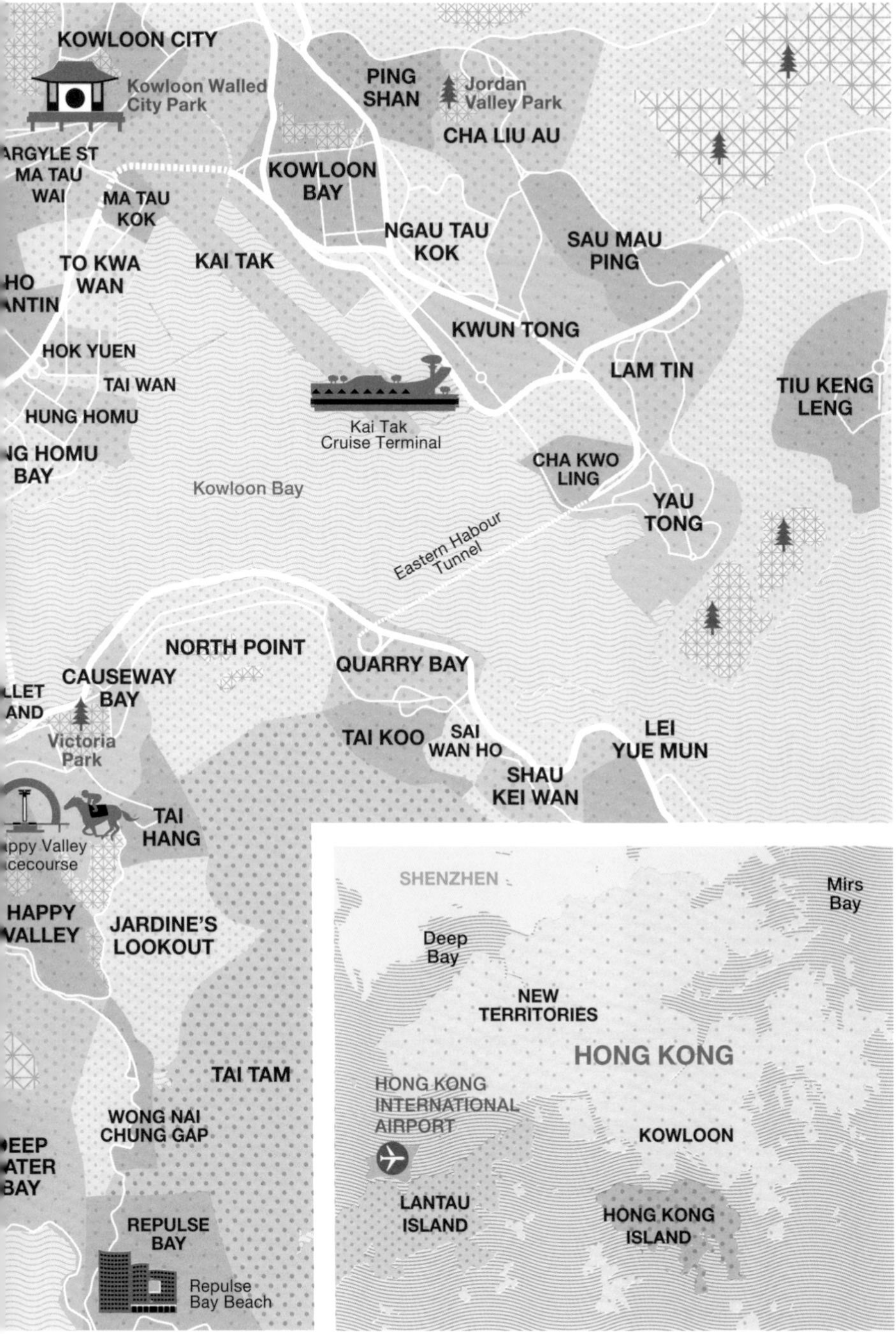
KOWLOON CITY
Kowloon Walled City Park
PING SHAN
Jordan Valley Park
CHA LIU AU
ARGYLE ST
MA TAU WAI
MA TAU KOK
KOWLOON BAY
NGAU TAU KOK
SAU MAU PING
TO KWA WAN
KAI TAK
HO
NTIN
KWUN TONG
LAM TIN
HOK YUEN
TAI WAN
TIU KENG LENG
HUNG HOMU
Kai Tak Cruise Terminal
G HOMU BAY
CHA KWO LING
Kowloon Bay
YAU TONG
Eastern Habour Tunnel
NORTH POINT
QUARRY BAY
CAUSEWAY BAY
LLET
AND
Victoria Park
TAI KOO
SAI WAN HO
LEI YUE MUN
SHAU KEI WAN
TAI HANG
ppy Valley
cecourse
HAPPY VALLEY
JARDINE'S LOOKOUT
TAI TAM
WONG NAI CHUNG GAP
EEP
ATER
BAY
REPULSE BAY
Repulse Bay Beach
SHENZHEN
Mirs Bay
Deep Bay
NEW TERRITORIES
HONG KONG
HONG KONG INTERNATIONAL AIRPORT
KOWLOON
LANTAU ISLAND
HONG KONG ISLAND

Need to know
Get to grips with the basics

Find your way around town, discover the ritual of breakfast dim sum and charm the locals with a few choice phrases in the native tongue. While Hong Kong is a city that welcomes visitors with open arms, it always helps to have a little insider wisdom. Read on for some key tips if you are visiting Hong Kong for the first time.

Quick Cantonese
Conversation

While you'll be able to get around Hong Kong with relative ease using only English, knowing a few key Cantonese phrases will come in handy (and may win you some respect). With nine tones, Cantonese is notoriously difficult to master; unlike Mandarin, it's impossible to translate it into the Roman alphabet and conversation is often reliant on slang words that change frequently. If you're going to remember one word make it "*Ng goy*", which can express gratitude or demand attention depending on the context. Use it to say "Thank you" to your taxi driver or shopkeeper and get a waiter's attention. Start the day with "*Jo san*", which means "Good morning". But after midday, switch over to "*Lei ho*", the common way of saying hello. (For more handy vocabulary tips, see the Resources section on page 138.)

One day I'll work out how to use my camera

Taxi tactics
Transport

Affordable and abundant, Hong Kong's taxis may not be the most charming in the world but they're an efficient way to get around the city.

Well, I can see Kowloon from here – but no taxis to take me there

Drivers' speed and frequent gruffness can sometimes be intimidating so be sure to wear your seatbelt and have small notes handy. The taxis you'll see most are red and based in Hong Kong and Kowloon. While these cars can go anywhere in the city, green taxis only operate in the New Territories and light-blue vehicles are restricted to Lantau Island. Sometimes it can be difficult to get cabs to take you across the harbour (from Hong Kong to Kowloon or vice versa), though a handy trick is to make an undulating wave-like shape with your hand when you hail one as this is code for crossing over. Also make sure you get in the correct line at taxi stands: some are designated for cross-harbour cars only. And try to avoid catching a cab between 15.00 and 16.00 as it's when drivers change their shifts.

Breakfast of champions
Dining

Morning dim sum is a popular occasion for extended families to get together. Dim sum places open as early as 05.00 and you'll often see groups of 10 people or more sharing food around a large circular table. It's an experience that is designed to be communal. Eating what you are offered is the polite thing to do and if you see people knocking on the table it's because this is an acceptable way of saying thank you for being served something.

The big smoke
Rites and rituals

Walk around the city for an afternoon and you'll likely come across the smell of incense burning. Scattered among gleaming new office towers and shopping malls, Hong Kong's temples are hubs for each community, where incense sticks and coils are lit to honour the dead and the gods. At certain times of year you may also see large piles of colourful paper being burned in metal cans on the street. Traditionally representing money, joss paper comes in many intricate designs so don't be affronted if it looks like someone is setting fire to a small sports car or Hermès Birkin bag – these are all just paper offerings to honour ancestors.

High ideals
Transport

There are few better airports to travel to and from than Hong Kong International Airport (*see essay on page 76*). While the terminals themselves are beacons of efficiency, the Airport Express train makes your journey easy before you even start. It only takes 24 minutes to get from the heart of town to the airport. Check-in desks at both Hong Kong and Kowloon stations allow you to drop your bags up to 24 hours before your flight departs, making early hotel check-out times or late dinner meetings a breeze.

Come rain or shine
Weather

The weather here can be as dramatic and changeable as the skyline. If you're caught without an umbrella, the city's myriad convenience stores always sell them. And during the summer, be sure to keep an extra layer in your bag as offices and shopping malls can be a little aggressive with their air conditioning.

Onward and upward
Development

You'll never be far from some sort of construction in Hong Kong. New MTR lines and gravity-defying apartment buildings seem to be in constant demand. In 2017, the world's largest underground station is set to be finished in West Kowloon and will bring an estimated 200,000 travellers to the city every day. On the island's southside, it's hard to miss the new MTR line being built. And if you have a window seat on your flight over, check out the huge road bridge underway to connect Macau and Hong Kong.

Dignified approach
Society

It'll come as no surprise that Hong Kong has tensions at various levels with mainland China. While you're unlikely to encounter these during your visit to the city, be sensitive to the pride that many people here take in their unique culture and history. Many identify themselves as Hong Kongers first and Chinese second.

Hello, will you be my friend? Hello? How rude...

Street life
Leisure

Hong Kong is home to hundreds of thousands of domestic workers, most of whom come from the Philippines and Indonesia. For the majority, their day off is Sunday and without living space of their own they take to the streets to relax. Hosting picnics, dance competitions, card games and even makeshift beauty salons, this group of women make the most of every inch of the city's parks, pavements and walkways. Ultimately a symptom of immigration mismanagement, such gatherings are an important, highly visible part of Hong Kong society.

Heavy lifting
Goods delivery

In some areas of Hong Kong you'll see old women pushing handcarts full of recycling along streets lined with luxury shops. These simple iron trays on wheels transport everything from mail and machinery to fresh produce and rubbish around the city. Although rough around the edges, these carts are incredibly useful on often steep and narrow backstreets. They're seemingly disorganised but actually highly efficient; just like much of Hong Kong.

Hotels
— New heights of hospitality

While not a city short on accommodation, Hong Kong's hotel scene can sometimes appear to be more about chains than charm. One look at the city's vertigo-inspiring skyline and you can't miss the names of the global hotel brands that have staked their claim to the towers they occupy. But as with many things in the city, the best options can be slightly harder to find.

With the following selection we've done the work for you. Alongside grand, historic flagship properties and the sleek, sky-high rooms that the city has become known for, newer and more intimate hotels are helping to give lesser-visited neighbourhoods a new identity.

From airy rooms that overlook a marina on the south side of Hong Kong Island to a design hotel just off the beaten track in east Kowloon, each of these hotels offer their own take on this busy city.

Well, I don't want to be late for my massage, do I?

①
The Upper House, Admiralty
East meets West

When it comes to mixing contemporary Asian and European design, no hotel in Hong Kong does it better than The Upper House. The hotel's discreet grey entrance was designed by British architect Thomas Heatherwick, while the interiors are by one of Hong Kong's most respected young architects: André Fu.

Originally built to house serviced apartments, rooms at The Upper House are large, especially for space-challenged Hong Kong. All are decorated with a relaxed palette and every room features a large bathroom with tubs positioned to look out over Hong Kong while you enjoy a soak.

Service at the hotel is top notch, with a smart and discreet team led by Swiss GM Marcel Thoma to handle everything from restaurant reservations to pre-packed picnics for a boating trip. And there are few better places in Hong Kong to grab a drink than one of the booths at Café Gray Deluxe, from where the entire city can be discussed over an Old Fashioned from the bar's specialist menu.
Pacific Place, 88 Queensway
+852 2918 1838
upperhouse.com

MONOCLE COMMENT: While the hotel may not have a pool or spa on the premises, the concierge can arrange for a number of services to be set up in your room. This includes a masseuse who will transform your space into your own private health club.

②
Mandarin Oriental, Central
Individual interiors

Hong Kong's Mandarin Oriental tells the story of the birth of the five-star Asian hospitality business. Built in 1963 as The Mandarin, the hotel was once the tallest building in Hong Kong (at 26 storeys, this is sadly no longer true) and, along with the Oriental in Bangkok, became a flagship property for the Mandarin Oriental hotel group.

Today the hotel is still one of the city's most luxurious options. Located in the heart of Central, it's as well known for its award-winning spa and restaurants as it is for its individually furnished rooms, which are decorated with reminders of the hotel's Asian heritage using ornaments, ceramics and textiles. Found on the 24th floor, the Mandarin Spa is home to a salon and the hotel's famous barbershop, as well as a pool, gym and nine treatment rooms.
5 Connaught Road
+852 2522 0111
mandarinoriental.com/hongkong

MONOCLE COMMENT: Among the rooms on offer you'll find the modern, bold Lichfield suite, the wood-panelled Howarth suite and the calm, Japanese-inspired Meiji suite.

③
The Pottinger, Central
Local design champion

This recently opened boutique hotel couldn't be better located for those wanting to experience the hustle and bustle of both old and new Hong Kong. Within walking distance are many of the city's most charming street markets, luxury shops and traditional restaurants.

The rooms reference old Hong Kong design and many display work by Fan Ho, who shot iconic images of the city during the 1950s and 1960s. There is a popular bar on the roof and a branch of Coco Espresso, one of the city's best coffee shops, can be found just down the road.
21 Stanley Street
+852 2308 3188
thepottinger.com

MONOCLE COMMENT: The Envoy roof bar at the hotel serves great cocktails mixed by Antonio Lai, the bartender behind the Quinary and Origin.

Airport pick-up options

01 **Helicopter, The Peninsula:** If you're in a real hurry there's no quicker way to get to the airport than by helicopter. Guests at The Peninsula can board via the hotel's Clipper Club lounge on the 30th floor straight onto a five-seater Aerospatiale Squirrel AS355N, which is equipped with comfy leather seats and a top sound system. If you're happier on the ground, The Peninsula's fleet of 14 Rolls-Royce Phantoms in the hotel's signature green is also a treat.
hongkong.peninsula.com

02 **BMW i3, The Upper House:** In a city where pollution is a problem, cars such as the electric BMW i3 should surely be more popular. Thankfully, the Upper House is leading the charge with this recent addition to its collection of hotel cars.
upperhouse.com

03 **London taxi, Grand Hyatt:** If you happen to see a traditional London taxi driving around Hong Kong, it's most likely to be ferrying a guest to or from the Grand Hyatt. Available to hire for any trips around the city, it's certainly more comfortable than the local taxis.
hongkong.grand.hyatt

04 **Toyota Alphard, Four Seasons:** If you're travelling with colleagues for business and need to get around in comfort, there are few better options than the Toyota Alphard. Able to carry six people, the Four Seasons' fleet also has wi-fi and digital-charging facilities onboard.
fourseasons.com/hongkong

Close quarters

Despite being on the Kowloon side of things, Hotel Icon is located minutes from the Cross-Harbour Tunnel. It takes you straight to Causeway Bay and is also a few minutes' walk from Hung Hom MTR Station.

Global blend
—
Icon's interior was created by a host of designers

④
Hotel Icon, Tsim Sha Tsui East
Kowloon pioneer

Central may have long been the financial core of Hong Kong but across the harbour a growing number of corporations and small firms are setting up in skyscrapers. Not least among said towers is the International Commerce Centre in Tsim Sha Tsui, which is the city's tallest building.

The opening of Hotel Icon in 2011 filled the absence of a well-run Kowloon boutique hotel that's perfect for business travellers. A selection of architects and artists from around the world contributed to the look and feel of the place: architect Rocco Yim designed the hotel's all-glass exteriors – which offer panoramic views of Victoria Harbour across all floors – while French botanist Patrick Blanc designed the indoor vertical garden that spans the hotel lobby.

The streamlined room interiors influenced by the Chinese philosophy of yin and yang also make for comforting sleep and work quarters. Owned by the Hong Kong Polytechnic University's hospitality school, Hotel Icon's top-notch service, breadth of restaurant offerings and harbour-side location make it one of our top picks in the city.
17 Science Museum Road
+852 3400 1000
hotel-icon.com

MONOCLE COMMENT: The hotel's club lounge, Above and Beyond, offers some of the city's finest Cantonese cuisine and dim sum with an inventive twist.

⑤
Grand Hyatt, Wan Chai
Made for business

Located right on the harbour front in the heart of Wan Chai, the Grand Hyatt is our top pick for those doing business in the city. Book one of the hotel's suites and you'll be treated to the services of one of the hotel's experienced team of butlers, who can unpack or pack your bags, arrange your itinerary in the city and be relied upon 24/7 during your stay.

The two-storey club lounge is looked after by a team of multilingual staff ready to assist, while cosy seating areas provide great spots for informal meetings (three private boardrooms are also available for something more structured). The hotel's 11th floor is one of the city's best-kept secrets. Home to the Plateau Spa, an outdoor running track, pool and well-equipped gym, it's a great place to tackle jet lag head on.
1 Harbour Road
+852 2588 1234
hongkonggrand.hyatt.com

MONOCLE COMMENT: The hotel's smart 16-seat teppanyaki restaurant, the Teppanroom, is a great place for working lunch with a colleague.

Show boat
Many of the Hyatt's rooms have harbour views

A good brew and a great view – what a way to beat jet lag

Warm welcome

If you haven't booked yourself a room at the Grand Hyatt you can still experience the hotel's peaceful 11th-floor terrace. Either book a treatment at the Plateau Spa or make a reservation for weekend brunch at The Grill, the hotel's poolside restaurant.

(6)

99 Bonham, Sheung Wan
Design-focused stay

Nestled in the heart of bustling Sheung Wan, 99 Bonham is just a stone's throw away from some of the city's best shops, galleries and historical sights.

Designed by Milan-based Antonio Citterio Patricia Viel and Partners, the apartment-style rooms are sharp and clean, decorated in a subtle palette of soft greys with touches of dark wood, rich marble tiling and fine textiles. Each one is set out as a mini guest suite with a well-stocked pantry, cosy lounge and dining area and a spacious workstation. Bathroom fixtures are (perhaps unsurprisingly) all Citterio pieces, while the bedding and linen come from Frette.

With only three units per floor, rooms at 99 Bonham are well sized. And with its subtle design and a rooftop terrace that can be booked for barbecues or private parties, 99 Bonham is a dependable choice for longer stays.

99 Bonham Strand
+852 3940 1111
99bonham.com

MONOCLE COMMENT: Just down the road from 99 Bonham are the hotel's sister properties, The Putman and The Jervois, both of which also make great design stays.

(7)

T Hotel, Pokfulam
Rooms with a view

T Hotel is Hong Kong's first student-operated training hotel, opened in 2011 by the Vocational Training Council. Set along the city's western fringe of Hong Kong Island, the hotel's green surroundings and hillside spot in Pokfulam also provide sweeping views of the South China Sea and the Peak. It's an area rarely explored by visitors but offers perfect access to both the city and Hong Kong's south side.

From the reception and the spa facilities to housekeeping and reservations, students run every aspect of the hotel, which gives them hands-on exposure to daily operations before graduating from their vocational courses. As the students only work for a month, the keen staff members have to be quick to pick up the ropes.

Although it is run as a training hotel it's hard to tell from the high quality of service. Guests can choose from western or Chinese dining options, make use of the business centre or book a massage at the spa. T Hotel's affordable rates make this hotel one of Hong Kong's hidden gems.

6F, VTC Pokfulam Complex,
145 Pokfulam Road
+852 3717 7388
thotel.edu.hk

MONOCLE COMMENT: The neighbourhood of Pokfulam is also home to one of the city's last remaining villages, which is about 300 years old.

Material gain

Expect wood, concrete and brickwork accents

(8)

Pentahotel, San Po Kong
Contemporary cool

Despite plenty of five-star hotels to choose from, Hong Kong doesn't have many well-designed places to stay that are aimed at a younger crowd. The recently opened Pentahotel looks set to change this. Found in a post-industrial neighbourhood near the new Kai Tak Cruise Terminal, the hotel's relaxed rooms feature reclaimed wood, aged brick and painted concrete walls.

At the heart of the hotel is the Penta lounge, a multifunctional space that houses the hotel lobby and an open marketplace-restaurant-bar-café space where guests can order Hong Kong street-food classics as well as simple western comfort food. On the ground floor an eat-in or takeaway pizza spot caters to both guests and neighbours. The games rooms just off the Penta lounge offer some R&R with pool tables, video games and table football, while an outdoor pool and a gym provide ample space for keeping fit.

Located a few minutes' walk from Diamond Hill MTR Station and up-and-coming neighbourhoods in Kowloon, it's the perfect place to explore Hong Kong's less-trodden path.
19 Luk Hop Street
+852 3112 8222
pentahotels.com

MONOCLE COMMENT: With a focus on affordable rooms, Pentahotel is a great option for groups of travellers.

New frontier

Diamond Hill was once home to thousands of squatter dwellings that were demolished. Today, with the development of Kowloon East and the Kai Tak Cruise Terminal, it's a neighbourhood with a very different identity.

⑨

Island Shangri-La, Admiralty
Retail respite

With the luxury stores of Pacific Place shopping mall on the hotel's doorstep and a range of restaurants within the building, the Island Shangri-La is our pick for a weekend of shopping. Just a short walk away is the peaceful Hong Kong Park, which is perfect for an early-morning jog, while the hotel's pool and 24-hour gym will help to keep you trim without leaving the building.

The hotel's 565 guestrooms and 34 suites are spacious and decorated with the same Asian focus as the entrance lobby that houses the largest Chinese landscape painting on silk in the world. Located on the hotel's 56th floor, French restaurant Petrus has one Michelin star and a good wine list. Summer Palace, with two Michelin stars, is a favourite for traditional Cantonese meals; the Lobster Bar & Grill, with its frequent live music, is great for an informal drink.

Pacific Road, Supreme Court Road
+852 2877 3838
shangri-la.com

MONOCLE COMMENT: Booking a Horizon Club room ensures access to a separate concierge team and the club lounge's roof garden, while a limousine service can also be arranged for an airport pick-up.

Sister act

Visitors have been known to end up at the wrong Shangri-La as the brand also operates a property on the other side of Victoria Harbour. Although slightly older, the Kowloon Shangri-La boasts stunning views of Hong Kong's skyline.

High ideals
This Chinese silk painting rises 16 floors

Hong Kong's old hotels

Developers haven't always been good at preserving or renovating older buildings in Hong Kong and the hotel business has seen its fair share of demolitions. Despite having only been in business for four years, the city's original Ritz-Carlton (today the hotel is housed at the top of the 118-floor International Commerce Centre) is still missed by many nostalgic Hong Kongers. Once occupying a 25-storey building in Central it was torn down in 2008 to make way for office space. Nearby was the 1970s Furama Hong Kong Hotel. Managed by the Inter-Continental group for a stint, it had a famous revolving restaurant on its top floor but was razed to be replaced with the AIA office tower.

Perhaps the most famous hotel to be destroyed was the Hong Kong Hilton, which stood on the site of today's Cheung Kong Centre in Central. The first five-star hotel to be built on Hong Kong Island, it was home to the Foreign Correspondents' Club during the 1960s, sailors and soldiers on leave and the city's notorious Dragon Boat Bar.

Reversing the trend of tearing down old structures, the Tai O Heritage Hotel on Lantau Island was opened in 2009. Its nine simple rooms are housed in a restored 1902 police station that was one of the first to be built on Hong Kong's outlying islands and originally focused on cracking down on the work of pirates. While it's not the most convenient location for urban exploration, it's a great place to escape for a break. There is also a restaurant with panoramic views over the sea.
taioheritagehotel.com

10

The Peninsula, Tsim Sha Tsui
Old-school appeal

There are few places in Hong Kong that can drum up the city's romance and history like The Peninsula, the iconic hotel that opened in 1928 overlooking Victoria Harbour from Kowloon's shoreline.

A daily queue forms in the lobby, with visitors wanting to experience the hotel's famous afternoon tea (tables can be reserved for guests). Outside, the forecourt still retains its original grandeur with the hotel's fleet of Rolls-Royce Phantoms.

Decorated in a neutral palette and outfitted with custom Cassina sofas and dining chairs from Poltrona Frau, the focus of the rooms is the view – which for most is out across the harbour.

The Peninsula's nine bars and restaurants include Gaddi's, a classic French restaurant, with silver service; there's also the traditionally Japanese Imasa and Spring Moon, which is one of the city's top spots for a dim-sum lunch.
Salisbury Road
+852 2920 2888
hongkong.peninsula.com

MONOCLE COMMENT: If you're a fan of chocolate, be sure to try some from the hotel's very own in-house chocolatier.

11

Ovolo, Aberdeen
Southern comforts

A local business success story, the Ovolo group was founded in Hong Kong in 2002 and now runs seven properties in the city and three in Australia. While it has a few locations closer to Central, the Aberdeen property is a great option for those wanting to wake up to sea views and experience life on the south side of the island.

The rooms are bright and fuss-free. It's a short cab ride from Stanley Market as well as the up-and-coming creative neighbourhood of Wong Chuk Hang and beaches at Deepwater Bay and Repulse Bay.
100 Shek Pai Wan Road
+852 3728 1000
ovolohotels.com

MONOCLE COMMENT: If you're keen to try a local brand but want to be closer to Central, check out the Ovolo Noho near Sheung Wan or the Ovolo Central just above Lan Kwai Fong.

Bare essentials — The East Hotel boasts minimalist interiors

⑫
The East Hotel, Taikoo Shing
Alternative view

While few travellers have had reason to visit Taikoo Shing in the past, this district on the eastern end of Hong Kong Island has grown into one of the city's up-and-coming business hubs. It was an area previously dominated by clusters of housing complexes but now an array of shops and restaurants has opened up, catering to the needs of its residents and visitors.

Conveniently erected adjacent to the Tai Koo MTR Station and a short drive from Central, the sleek East Hotel is an ideal option for business travellers. All rooms have been upholstered with light wood and minimalist furnishings, while the large windows keep the rooms bright and offer stunning views of the city.

After a long day of work or sightseeing, rooftop bar Sugar offers a menu of light snacks and tasty cocktails to help you unwind. Plus, Sugar's outdoor patio has one of the best views in the city, overlooking East Kowloon.
29 Taikoo Shing Road
+852 3968 3968
east-hongkong.com

MONOCLE COMMENT: The perfect place to stay for anyone with meetings east of Causeway Bay.

Food and drink
City bites

It's no secret that Hong Kong is a great city to eat your way around. From Michelin-starred fine dining to family-run food stalls, the city's restaurants, bars and cafés form an important part of daily life. Many Hong Kongers live in small apartments with limited space for cooking and eating so you'll regularly see large groups of friends and family members dining out together.

Over the past few years the restaurant scene has exploded. Today you'll find independent streetside places that specialise in paella or fried chicken alongside restaurants showcasing all forms of traditional Chinese staples, from mouth-numbing Sichuan spice to more comforting Cantonese dishes.

We'll show you some of the city's most popular hotspots, serving dishes from all around the world. We have also dedicated some pages to authentic and local specialities (and how to order them).

Restaurants
Fine dining

① Yardbird, Sheung Wan
Feeling peckish?

Having opened its doors in 2011, there's rarely a night when Yardbird isn't packed. The atmospheric, no-reservations *yakitori-ya* (a traditional Japanese grilled chicken outlet) is now a popular staple of the Hong Kong food scene. Run by Canadian chef Matt Abergel and his charismatic team, the restaurant orders chickens on a daily basis from a New Territories farm in order to not waste anything.

With a selection of sakés, whiskies and cocktails you won't mind the wait in the bar for your table. What follows is a menu of fresh skewers – using everything from thigh and breast to heart and skin – that sells out nightly. Sides such as Korean fried cauliflower go almost as quickly as the *yakitori*. Doors open at 18.00, except Sunday; turn up early to get your name on the list.
33-35 Bridges Street
+852 2547 9273
yardbirdrestaurant.com

Yard sale

Many of the team at Yardbird worked together before the restaurant's opening. In fact, a group of them went into business together to set up Sunday's Grocery (*see page 31*) to offer their famous chicken in a takeaway setting.

Chicken supreme
'Yakitori' is now a Hong Kong staple

❷
Tate Dining Room and Bar, Central
Appetising and artistic

Soho's busy Elgin Street may not be the first place you'd head for a quiet dining experience. But walk past the busy bars and restaurants that line its lower level and head to Tate Dining Room and Bar, an intimate 26-seater opened by Vicky Lau in 2012. Originally a graphic designer, Lau pays as much attention to the feel and presentation of her food as she does its taste.

Lau designs and illustrates the accompanying menu herself. A light herbal consommé is poured from a glass teapot over an oyster shell containing a Gillardeau oyster, beef tongue and *kimchi*-pickled daikon. Meanwhile, her famous Zen Garden dessert places individual macarons, cakes and marshmallows in a Japanese rock garden, equipped with a miniature rake.

59 Elgin Street
+852 2555 2172
tate.com.hk

I'm as good at pouring as I am at pawing

③
208, Sheung Wan
Gather around

Historically a street lined with antiques shops and coffin-makers, Hollywood Road is now home to some of the city's best bars and restaurants. Opened in 2010, 208 Duecento Otto was an early arrival. Designed by Istanbul's Autoban, the space is divided into a restaurant upstairs and a bar on the ground floor opening onto the street. The traditional Neapolitan pizzas are one of the main reasons to go. Order one at the bar to share with a bottle from 208's Italian wine list for an afternoon of people-watching.

208 Hollywood Road
+852 2549 0208
208.com.hk

Fun in a bun

Burgers at The Butchers Club hit the spot

❹

The Butchers Club, Wan Chai

What's your beef?

Hong Kong has no shortage of burger joints – and there's also no clear-cut answer as to which is the best in town. But if you're craving a juicy tried-and-tested burger while in the city, you would be well advised to go for one of those offered by The Butchers Club.

The restaurant is part of an empire of beef-related establishments of the same name, including a butchery, private dining space and deli. What sets The Butchers Club apart from other grillers is its eye for detail. Each patty is freshly ground from grain-fed Australian Angus beef, while the thick-cut fries are cooked in duck fat for that extra bite of richness. Eating these flavoursome burgers can be a messy business but they certainly hit the spot.

GF, Rialto Building,
2 Landale Street
+852 2552 8281
butchersclub.com.hk

Meat and greet

If you're in Wong Chuk Hang, stop by The Butchers Club Deli: a New York-style deli by day and a butchery and private dining room at night. It is on the 16th floor of the Shui Ki Industrial Building at 18 Wong Chuk Hang Road.
butchersclub.com.hk

⑤
Sushi Sase, Central
Fruits of the sea

Given the city's love for Japanese cuisine it's no surprise that Hong Kong has countless conveyor-belt sushi restaurants and ramen joints. But for those seeking a unique and understated experience, Sushi Sase is worth a visit.

The *kaiseki* approach at Sushi Sase means the menu selection is decided by chef Satoshi Sase, who worked at Japan's Sushi Zen in Sapporo. Offerings change daily depending on the produce that is flown in from the Tsukiji fish market in Tokyo.

Impeccable attention to detail – the design features beautiful wood and a light colour palette – carefully reflects the restaurant's Japanese influences. With a soothing atmosphere and the finest seafood on offer, Sushi Sase is one of the city's top Japanese dining establishments.
UGF, Hilltop Plaza,
49 Hollywood Road
+852 2815 0455

Big in Japan
Sushi Sase's fish is flown fresh from Tokyo

⑥
Hong Kee Congee, Tai Hang
Quick breakfast

Operating on one of Tai Hang's quiet streets, the family-run Hong Kee has cooked up some of the best congee in the city for decades. The grandfather of the family is up at dawn to make rice rolls at the front of the shop while his grandson helps out after school. Its reputation draws some of the city's most successful restaurateurs for bowls of congee: Chinese rice porridge that can be eaten at any time of day and in many variations, with toppings such as century egg and pork. Pull up a stool, ask for the English menu and enjoy a bowl for about HK$8.
11 King Street

Must-try
Fried chicken from Sunday's Grocery, Kennedy Town
This twice-fried chicken is a great reason to jump on the tram or MTR and head to Kennedy Town. Buy a box of either the original or Korean-style chicken and a bottle of Japanese beer to wash it down. Designed as a takeaway-sandwich and chicken shop, Sunday's Grocery also stocks a wide selection of Japanese whisky and homeware. You can pull up a crate outside to chow down or take your food to the nearby waterfront.
sundaysgrocery.com

7

Ho Lee Fook, Central
Chinese cuisine with a twist

After cutting his teeth in some of Sydney's finest establishments, including Marque and Ms G's, Taiwanese-Canadian chef Jowett Yu (*pictured*) is in Hong Kong to explore his version of modern Chinese cuisine with his restaurant Ho Lee Fook.

A windowless basement below the kitchen throngs with a fashionable young crowd but it would be wrong to view the place as a flash in the hipster pan. Comfortably weaving in and out of Asia's many culinary traditions, Yu's food is at once familiar and innovative. It's essentially a Chinese restaurant but you wouldn't want to miss the *sambal* that comes with the fried chicken wings or the wagyu short rib with kimchi and jalapeño purée. Obsessed with Chinese cooking, Yu can be found roaming the wet markets each day for fresh seasonal ingredients.

1-5 Elgin Street
+852 2810 0860
holeefook.com.hk

⑧
Otto e Mezzo Bombana, Central
Taste of Tuscany

Following the closure of Toscana restaurant in 2008, chef Umberto Bombana stayed in Hong Kong to open Otto e Mezzo (named after Federico Fellini's classic film *8 ½*). It offers a menu where quality ingredients take centre stage in classic and contemporary Tuscan-inspired dishes. Some of Bombana's best-known servings are only available during white-truffle season between November and December. The cosy bar is an ideal spot for a pre-dinner tipple.
Shop 202, Landmark Alexandra,
18 Chater Road
+852 2537 8859
ottoemezzobombana.com

Must-try
Pork belly bao from Little Bao, Sheung Wan
Think of the *bao* as Asia's answer to the burger. This hearty bun is filled with slow-braised pork belly that's topped with a *shiso*-garnished salad, sesame dressing and hoisin ketchup.
little-bao.com

Fine dining

Dinner at Amber is an indulgent affair

Hooked on a feeling

At Amber you'll be eating beneath a striking Adam Tihany-designed chandelier where over 4,000 brass rods are suspended from the ceiling. There are also two private dining rooms that house Amber's extensive wine collection in their glass walls.

⑨
Amber, Central
Dinner to impress

Arguably the city's first homegrown modern European fine diner to make an international impact, the restaurant led by Richard Ekkebus in the Landmark Mandarin Oriental has gone from strength to strength since opening in 2005. From breakfast to lunch on weekdays, it's not uncommon to see the Adam Tihany-designed dining room filled with suits (but don't let that frighten you).

Dinner is a more indulgent affair with an eight-course degustation on offer, as well as a five-course menu and à la carte. An elaborate lunch menu is available on weekends. With Ekkebus's Dutch upbringing and experience in the tropics (Barbados and Mauritius) via France, expect influences from around the world with Japan at the forefront. The dishes change according to the season but the Hokkaido sea urchin with lobster Jell-O is something of a modern classic.

Drinks are central to the experience too, with pairings on set menus designed by sommelier John Chan. Inside the wine cellar is a private room for those wanting a more intimate experience. The restaurant also has an impressive pop-up guest-chef calendar, attracting top names from around the globe into its kitchens. For these special sessions or even regular dining, book well ahead.
7F, The Landmark Mandarin Oriental, The Landmark,
15 Queen's Road
+852 2132 0066
amberhongkong.com

Must-try
Prawn wonton noodles from Mak's Noodle, Central
These small bowls of noodles and handmade prawn wontons are so moreish that you may want to order two. This family-run business has been making its famous dish for three generations. Perfectly cooked noodles are served in a tasty light broth with a generous helping of plump prawn dumplings that are wrapped in a thin wonton skin. The wontons and serving size may be smaller than you expect but their flavour is unbeatable.
77 Wellington Street

(10)
Tsui Wah, Central
Convenience cuisine

Most Hong Kongers will have grabbed a late-night bowl of fish-ball noodles at Tsui Wah. First opened in 1967 in Kowloon as a basic *bing sutt* café serving coffee, tea and baked goods, Tsui Wah expanded during the 1980s into one of the best known chains of *cha chaan teng* (restaurants offering Asian and western dishes). The 30 or so Tsui Wah locations across Hong Kong and beyond serve everything from pasta to Hong Kong toast with condensed milk. The Wellington Street branch is open 24 hours a day.
GF-2F, 15-19 Wellington Street
+852 2525 6338
tsuiwah.com

(11)
Grassroots Pantry & Prune, Sai Ying Pun
Healthy breakfast

After a few too many late nights, a breakfast at Prune Organic Deli is a good idea. Located in a quiet cul-de-sac in Sai Ying Pun, the café's plant-filled terrace is the perfect place to read the papers over a healthy breakfast. Chef Peggy Chan (*pictured*) has an all-day menu that includes fresh juices, home-roasted granola and a refreshing acai berry bowl. Those after something more substantial should order the eggs *en cocotte* or lemon chia-seed waffle. Next door is Grassroots Pantry, Chan's restaurant.
12-14 Fuk Sau Lane
+852 2873 3353
grassrootspantry.com

Meat-free treat

Grassroots Pantry serves vegetarian food that even the most carnivorous of diners will find satisfying. Its take on Vietnamese *bun cha* includes honey-grilled hedgehog mushrooms and an almond-sesame dressing.

Relaxed affair
—
Common Ground does fine comfort food

⑫
Common Ground, Sheung Wan
LA vibe

While neighbourhood cafés serving tasty salads and good coffee are common in cities such as New York or Sydney, these kind of places are rare in Hong Kong. Tucked away on a set of stairs connecting bustling Soho with the residential Mid-Levels, Common Ground café fits the bill.

Having studied in LA, twin brothers Caleb and Joshua Ng (*both pictured, Joshua on left*) wanted to create a laidback restaurant reminiscent of those on the US West Coast. The menu features comfort-food dishes, hearty soups and signature scrambled eggs on toast. The Ng brothers also take pride in their coffee, made from three beans all roasted in Hong Kong. In a corner of the café the team maintains a retail outlet with an array of products, including enamelware from British brand Falcon and local honey.
19 Shing Wong Street
+852 2818 8318

On short trips you need to pack everything in

⑬
Ronin, Central
More than a bar

Although referred to as an *izakaya* (a traditional Japanese bar), to suggest that Ronin is a pub offering after-work libations and nibbles does the venue an injustice. This sliver of space hidden behind an unmarked sliding door has only 14 seats (plus a dozen standing spaces), making it one of the hardest tables in the city to book.

Despite its obvious debt to Japanese cuisine and focus on seafood, Ronin isn't a sushi restaurant either. That said, raw fish dishes such as *saba* (mackerel) sashimi do feature among the likes of grilled glazed triggerfish, and lightly seared Kagoshima beef served with egg yolk and maitake mushrooms.

The menu is divided into "smaller" and "bigger" sections, which serve more to describe the boldness of flavour than the size of the dish. If you can't decide, the generous tasting menu will let you try the restaurant's signatures and seasonal specials.

Like any good *izakaya*, the drinks are as important as the food. As well as being the first place in Hong Kong to serve the cult Japanese beer Hitachino Nest on draft, Ronin also offers hard-to-find whiskies, wines and sakés, not to mention house-infused shochus. Book well in advance for a seat but if you're looking to swing by for an after-dinner cocktail, try your luck at the standing bar.
8 On Wo Lane
+852 2547 5263
roninhk.com

Dumpling delight
Din Tai Fung also has a branch in Kowloon

(14)

Din Tai Fung, Causeway Bay
Delectable dumplings

Din Tai Fung started in the Taiwanese capital of Taipei in 1958 but Hong Kongers have since heartily embraced it as one of their very favourite places for a dumpling moment.

No visit to the restaurant would be complete without sampling its beloved signature dish: the delectable *xiao long bao*. A Shanghainese steamed-pork dumpling, each soup parcel is intricately folded 18 times before it's cooked in bamboo steamers. Ask the staff to show you the best way to enjoy the dumplings; generous helpings of Chinese black vinegar and ginger are key.

While Din Tai Fung may be best known for dumplings, it also serves an array of cold appetisers, speciality noodles including a Taiwanese braised-beef-soup variety and a selection of Chinese desserts such as red-bean-paste buns. We recommend arriving early to avoid queues or stopping by for a mid-afternoon snack. Even if there seems to be a wait, the restaurant's efficient staff and seating system mean you won't be standing around for too long.
Shop 3-11, 68 Yee Wo Street
+852 3160 8998
dintaifung.com.hk

Dining lesson

To get the best out of these famous 'xiao long bao' you have to eat them properly. Holding the dumpling in your spoon, pierce the skin with your chopsticks so the juice runs out. Garnish with the vinegar and soy-drenched ginger from the small dish and enjoy.

Small cafés
Size matters

1

ABC Kitchen, Sheung Wan
That's amore

Cooked-food centres are an important part of Hong Kong life. Most often found on the floor above wet markets, these stalls are lively and informal. At the Queen Street market you'll find a surprising option: tasty Italian food from ABC Kitchen. From pasta to wagyu-beef cheeks, this is a real high-low dining experience.
2F, Queen Street Cooked Food Market

2

Sing Heung Yuen, Central
Working lunch

Everyone comes here for one dish: beef-and-tomato-soup macaroni. Although Sing Heung Yuen has a proper kitchen, the dining area is built as a makeshift structure covered with tarpaulin and canvas – and no air-conditioning. Avoid office lunch hours when workers from Central's skyscrapers descend. An English menu is available.
2 Mee Lun Street

3

Australia Dairy Company, Jordan
Cracking fare

Arguably the most famous *cha chaan teng* in the city (it even has an English name), locals and visitors flock to this tea restaurant chiefly to try two dishes with a common theme: scrambled eggs and variations of the egg custard pudding. Don't be alarmed by the brusque service – it's all part of the charm.
47-49 Parkes Street

4

Man Wah, Hung Hom
Past times

Step into Man Wah and you will be transported back to the 1950s. The decor looks unchanged since it first opened while the café's menu, offering warm pineapple buns with butter and *yuen yeung* (Hong Kong-style milk tea mixed with coffee), is characteristic of Hong Kong's unique food culture.
2 Bulkeley Street

5

Cheung Fat, Sham Shui Po
Hidden delights

Off the beaten track in Sham Shui Po, Yiu Tung Street is home to many of Hong Kong's remaining *dai pai dongs* (open-air food stalls). In particular, Cheung Fat is one of the oldest noodle shops in the city, specialising in Cantonese-style noodle dishes. Cheung Fat's owner still follows traditional cooking techniques.
1 Yiu Tung Street

6

Man Sing, Tai Hang
Resident favourite

On the main thoroughfare of Tai Hang is Man Sing, a restaurant-cum-*dai pai dong* popular with locals. The daily menu is written in Chinese on an orange plastic board but there are some servers who can speak minimal English. It's best known for stacked meat patties topped with a salty egg yolk.
16 Wun Sha Street

Don't panic

A little rough around the edges in terms of both decor and service, these local cafés are among the most authentic dining experiences available in Hong Kong. Don't be put off by any initial language difficulties: there's often an English menu or friendly waiter to help.

7

Mido Café, Yau Ma Tei
Cinematic backdrop

Much loved by the city's directors and actors for its well-preserved interiors, little has changed here since the 1960s. The Mido Café has been the backdrop for many Hong Kong films, photo shoots and TV shows. Don't miss the restaurant's slightly unusual signature dish: baked spare-ribs rice.
63 Temple Street
+852 2384 6402

⑧
Wai Kee, Sham Shui Po
Pork life

Wai Kee won't win anyone over with its decor but it's the place to go for pork-liver noodles. Pork liver may not be for everyone but if you're feeling adventurous, head to the noodle shop on Fuk Wing Street or its secondary location on Pei Ho Street.
62-67 Fuk Wing Street and
165-167 Pei Ho Street
+852 2387 6515

9
Hoi On Café, Sheung Wan
Worthwhile journey

Stepping into Hoi On you will find traditional wooden booths that are characteristic of Hong Kong cafés of the past. It was opened in the 1950s and then-owner Mr Au Yeung decided to call it *hoi on*, meaning "safe voyage" in Chinese; it is his daughter Annie who now runs the café. We recommend the French toast.
17 Connaught Road

10
Lau Sam Kee, Sham Shui Po
Press to impress

Lau Sam Kee is one of few Hong Kong restaurants that still makes noodles using a bamboo press. Signature dishes include the springy wanton noodles in soup or a drier variety of noodle that is tossed in sauce. Visit the shop at Kweilin Street or its other spot on Fuk Wing Street.
48 Kweilin Street and
80 Fuk Wing Street

⑪
Sing Kee, Central
Quick bite

Nestled at the end of Stanley Street in a cluster of *dai pai dongs*, Sing Kee is arguably the most famous in Central. Fresh ingredients are kept near the hot stove carts, where dishes are prepared at a rapid rate. Ask the waiter for the daily specials as the best dishes are often off-menu.
9-10 Stanley Street
+852 2541 5678

Local flavour
Dim-sum restaurants

①
Lin Heung Lau, Central
Authentic dining

Established in 1926, Lin Heung Lau is among Hong Kong's oldest teahouses and dim sum is prepared here using the most traditional recipes and techniques. While Lin Heung Lau is far from modern and makes little effort to cater to non-Cantonese diners, Hong Kongers of all ages flock to the restaurant for its dim sum served in bamboo steamers.

Don't rely on the uniformed staff to come to your table with their carts laden high with food; chances are your fellow diners will have cleared the cart before you can get anything.

Despite the seemingly chaotic pace of dining, this dim sum institution is an authentic Hong Kong experience; endeavour to make friends with a fluent Cantonese speaker so you can enjoy it yourself.
160-164 Wellington Street
+852 2544 4556

After this I'll think about trying the dessert trolley

②
Yan Toh Heen, Tim Sha Tsui
Modern dim sum with a view

Although most visitors to the city tend to stay on Hong Kong Island, it's Kowloon that provides the iconic, postcard-perfect view of Victoria Harbour. Yan Toh Heen provides a ringside seat of this stunning cityscape while offering the chance to savour some of the best Cantonese food in town. At lunch, dim sum reigns supreme: if you're dining alone the seafood dumpling trio – grouper, crab leg and scallop – is a particularly good choice. Don't miss the soy sauce, an exclusive blend made by the Kowloon Soy Company. For dinner try the glossy, crisp slices of Peking duck served with nine homemade sauces and be sure to bring along plenty of hungry companions.

Following a refurbishment in 2013 by renowned hotel designer Chhada Siembieda Leung, the restaurant has the sophisticated feel of a contemporary Chinese home. It's the perfect environment for sinking into a plush banquette and sipping one of the many fine Chinese teas on the extensive beverage menu.
18 Salisbury Road
+852 2313 2323
hongkong-ic.intercontinental.com

❸
Lei Garden, Wan Chai
Award-winning chain

It's noteworthy that in a city as small as Hong Kong, Lei Garden has managed to expand to 10 locations since opening in 1973. Not only has it picked up several Michelin-starred accolades over the years, it is also celebrated as a favourite for Cantonese food.

Of Lei Garden's several locations we would recommend the Wan Chai one as the best. Apart from its dim-sum selection, the classic double-boiled soups and *siu yuk* (Chinese suckling pig) are particularly popular among the regulars.
326-338 Hennessy Road
+852 2892 0333
leigarden.hk

Dim-sum etiquette
Dim sum is served as early as 05.00 in Hong Kong, when you'll find locals ordering their favourite dishes for breakfast. While there is no exact way to enjoy it, here are a few pointers with regards etiquette.

Do:
01 When someone serves tea, tap your knuckles on the table, a gesture to mimic the act of bowing.
02 Prop the lid of a teapot open or turn it over altogether if you want to let the staff know you need a refill.
03 Feel free to order dessert or sweet dishes in the middle of a meal.
04 Leave a tip; service is rarely included.

Don't:
01 In general, don't flag down any waiter when you need something. Servers are assigned to look after you so take an early note of who yours is.
02 Never serve yourself tea first: always pour for other diners before yourself.
03 Don't take the last piece of dim sum without asking others. Cut dishes into smaller pieces if there are more people than the amount of food ordered.
04 Don't go to a dim-sum restaurant and order coffee: it's very much frowned upon.
05 Don't expect chilli-laden dishes. If you'd like to add a bit of a kick to your food, ask for *lak jiu jeung* (chilli paste).
06 When there are two sets of chopsticks at the table, don't use your own to pick up food. The second pair is intended as a sharing utensil.

④
Man Mo Café, Sheung Wan
High-end fusion

Nestled near the famous Man Mo Temple is Man Mo Café. Bringing a French twist to traditional dim sum, Swiss-born chef Nicolas Elalouf has teamed up with a duo of chefs (respectively from Robuchon and the famed Din Tai Fung restaurant) to create a menu of delectable dishes.

Traditional dim sum is given a modern twist: *xiao long bao* buns (typically a soup dumpling with pork filling) here boast a foie gras filling, while the Hong Kong-style egg tart *daan tat* has been tweaked with a lemon-curd filling and topped with meringue.
40 Upper Lascar Row
+852 2644 5644

❺
Maxim's Palace at City Hall, Central
Meals on wheels

While the decor errs on the side of kitsch, Maxim's Palace at City Hall is a fun experience for dim sum. Although many restaurants have abandoned the use of trollies to cart around dishes, the tradition holds here. Each cart comes with signs listing the dishes in English and Chinese, while some even have screens with images of the corresponding dishes. Reservations aren't accepted but try to get a seat by the window, where the restaurant has sweeping views of Victoria Harbour and looks over to Tsim Sha Tsui in Kowloon.
2F, Low Block, City Hall
+852 2521 1303

I'll get a taxi back rather than flying

Popular dim sum

01 **Char siu bao:** barbecued pork-filled steam buns
02 **Cheung fun:** steamed rice rolls that are generally filled with shrimp, beef or barbecued pork
03 **Fun guo:** *chiuchow*-style dumpling filled with peanuts, ground pork, dried shrimp and mushrooms
04 **Fung zao:** chicken feet in black-bean sauce
05 **Har gau:** prawn dumplings
06 **Lo bak go:** steamed or pan-fried radish cake
07 **Lo mai gai:** steamed sticky rice with chicken in a lotus leaf wrap
08 **Ma lai go:** steamed brown-sugar sponge cake
09 **Ngau yuk kao:** steamed beef balls
10 **Siu mai:** pork with prawn dumplings
11 **Zha leung:** Chinese fried dough in rice rolls

Bars
In good spirits

Secret bars

001 is one of the city's few speakeasies

①
001, Central
Hidden gem

Graham Street in Central is home to one of the city's oldest wet markets; street stalls have lined these narrow slopes for more than 150 years. But amid the frenetic atmosphere of the marketplace, with vendors selling everything from cooking sauces to butchered meats, it's easy to overlook the black frontage of an unassuming building that's often masked by crates of food. In the evenings its unmarked door, complete with illuminated bell, is in fact the entrance to 001, one of the city's first and only speakeasy bars.

Owners Emily Chiang and Alan Lin first moved to Hong Kong after several years in New York. On arriving they felt the lack of those cosy yet exclusive drinking dens that are so popular in New York.

In a nod to the speakeasies of the 1920s, Chiang and Lin designed 001 to be a place in the centre of the city where busy Hong Kongers could escape and relax. British designer Alexi Robinson (who previously worked for Tom Dixon) fitted the space with wide leather armchairs, an elegant black marble bar and intimate velvet booths, while Hong Kong design brand Latitude 22N contributed with branding and smaller touches such as the lighting.

A seating-only venue, 001 has a fine cocktail menu that is redesigned and updated by Chiang and bar manager Joanna Kent twice a year to make use of seasonal ingredients. A selection of spirits such as the Yamazaki Puncheon (a Japanese whisky aged in a 480ltr puncheon cask) and Oxley gin (distilled at minus 5C) can also only be found here. All syrups, juices and infused alcohols are made in-house to ensure utmost quality. Come the end of the evening you may well find yourself not wanting to venture outside again.

97 Wellington Street (entrance is the black door on Graham Street between Wellington and Stanley Streets)
+852 2810 6969

Coffee shops

01 Coco Espresso, Wan Chai: Monocle's Hong Kong bureau would have far slower mornings were it not for the team at Coco Espresso on Wan Chai's Anton Street. With four outlets in the city, Coco Espresso roasts its own beans at its café in Kowloon West. With friendly baristas, great-tasting coffee and additional shops on Stanley Street and Queen's Road Central, there are few better places to start the day.
cocobarista.com

02 Fuel, Central: Conveniently located in the IFC and Landmark shopping malls, Fuel's two outlets provide coffee, unfussy baked goods and charming service. Offering a stack of newspapers and good seating, they're the perfect place for a mid-shop pick-me-up.
fuelespresso.com

03 Barista Jam, Sheung Wan: One of Hong Kong's first independent specialist coffee shops, Barista Jam on Sheung Wan's Jervois Street sells coffee and simple food as well as beans, espresso machines and every tool a coffee-lover might need.
baristajam.com.hk

Bars with a view

01 Café Gray Deluxe, Central: There are few better places from which to admire Hong Kong than the 49th floor bar in the Upper House hotel. Reserve a corner table for views of Kowloon and order one of the bar's Old Fashioned cocktails.
cafegrayhk.com

02 Ozone, Kowloon: The highest bar in the world is at the Ritz-Carlton above Kowloon station. Designed by Japan's Wonderwall, the extravagant space matches the absurdity of the view from 490 metres above sea level.
ritzcarlton.com

03 Sevva, Central: From the large wraparound terrace at Sevva, Bonnae Gokson's rooftop bar and restaurant, the city's history can be charted from the Cenotaph in Statue Square to the Norman Foster-designed HSBC building.
sevva.hk

② Duddell's, Central
Rooftop respite

This beautiful two-storey space designed by Ilse Crawford houses a Chinese restaurant, art gallery and salon for cultural events. But above all it's a civilised spot for sundowners, especially the leafy terrace on the upper floor. The bar offers an impressive list of wines and spirits and a short-but-sharp selection of cocktails with playful Asian touches. The herbalist's mojito takes inspiration from traditional Chinese medicine and the Hong Konger, with plum wine, is the bar's own take on the New Yorker.

Members of Duddell's are granted privileges such as the ability to reserve a table at the bar and terrace. That said, a good concierge should be able to assist, and walk-ins are also welcome if there is room.
3F, Shanghai Tang Mansion,
1 Duddell Street
+852 2525 9191
duddells.co/home/en

③ Ping Pong 129, Sai Ying Pun
Gin palace

Behind a red door in Sai Ying Pun, stairs descend into a double-height space that was once a ping-pong club and is now a Spanish-style ginotería. With around 50 different types of gin, manager Juan Martínez Gregorio will change how you think of the simple G&T.
129 Second Street,
LG Nam Cheong House
pingpong129.com

④ Tai Lung Fung, Wan Chai
Vintage venue

Named after a 1960s Cantonese opera troupe, this bar pays homage to a bygone era. Interiors are modelled after Hong Kong's postwar boom with details including mosaic tile flooring, vintage movie posters and a plethora of knick-knacks emblematic of Hong Kong in the 1960s and 1970s.
The Archive, 5-9 Hing Wan Street
+852 2572 0055

⑤ Aberdeen Street Social, Central
Green space

The ground-floor bar of chef Jason Atherton's restaurant in the restored PMQ building opens onto a quiet tree-covered lawn. With a winning selection of beers and cocktails, it's a welcome spot of calm in the midst of busy Hong Kong.
35 Aberdeen Street
+852 2866 0300
aberdeenstreetsocial.hk

6

Butler, Tsim Sha Tsui
Bygone Japanese style

Butler transports you to an old-world Japanese bar, reminiscent of Tokyo's finest drinking establishments. With several years of experience at Ginza's best cocktail bars, Japanese owner Masayuki Uchida wanted to create a space that provided the best in Japanese bartending culture. At Butler the details count: more than 200 different spirits line the shelves, while Uchida and staff are all dressed in white dinner jackets.

While the leather-bound menu features an expansive list of cocktails and a selection of Japanese-influenced snacks, Uchida will also build drinks depending on a customer's palate. Despite its location just shy of East Tsim Sha Tsui's strip of rowdy bars, this quiet 20-seater den prides itself on meticulously made drinks and thoughtful service.
5F, 30 Mody Road
+852 2724 3828

Bite size

Butler may not be the best place to go if you're craving a full meal but it does offer small snacks, such as a simple cheese-and-charcuterie plate. Other items include a daily pasta dish, a wagyu-beef *tataki*, salads and rillettes of beef or sardine.

Teas, tonics and tofu

01 Leung Cha, Central: An age-old custom in Hong Kong, herbal teas are the remedy of choice when coming down with various illnesses. Brewed from a variety of medicinal herbs, different mixtures offer different remedies. These traditional shops serve a wide range of health tonics and brews and can still be found across Hong Kong. Some supermarkets will even stock them in plastic bottles. Two of the city's most beloved shops can be found in Central: Kung Lee and the 100-year-old Good Spring Company.
Kung Lee: Hollywood Road; Good Spring Company: Cochrane Street

02 Teakha, Sheung Wan: Housed in a shophouse on a quiet street in Sheung Wan, Teakha is a welcome surprise for tea-lovers. The menu features a range of drinks including masala chai and a speciality drink of *keemun* tea with red-date honey. Homemade pastries such as the signature green-tea cheesecake, scones and chiffon cakes are all must-tries.
teakha.com

03 Kung Wo Soya Bean Factory, Sham Shui Po: Founded in 1893, this century-old shop is famed for its soya bean treats. At Kung Wo, tofu is still proudly made using manually operated devices rather than modern-day machinery. Every day around 900kg of soya beans are processed to make an array of products, including a delicious soya-bean milk.
67 Fuk Lo Tsun Road

7
Salon No 10, Central
Dance the night away

This bar-cum-restaurant-cum-nightclub looks like nothing else in Hong Kong. Situated on a street above the busy clubland of Lan Kwai Fong, Salon No 10's interior feels part-nautical, part-domestic. Comfy banquettes and vintage furniture surround an open kitchen and bar.

A great place to grab a quiet drink early in the evening, it becomes a popular destination for the city's chic party-goers as the night goes on. Often host to guest DJs, this is an ideal spot for those who are in search of a little well-heeled nightlife.
10 Arbuthnot Road
+852 2801 6768

8
MO Bar, Central
Afternoon remedy

If you've exhausted yourself with some intensive shopping and are in need of a pick-me-up, your best bet is to grab an afternoon G&T at the MO Bar, the Landmark Mandarin Oriental's spacious ground-floor drinking den. All the syrups and infusions are made in-house and its fruit juices are squeezed daily. There's also a good selection of teas and coffees. In addition to the small plates that sit perfectly alongside the drinks, the bar hosts a famous lobster-and-champagne lunch every Sunday.
GF, The Landmark Mandarin Oriental, 15 Queen's Road
+852 2132 0188
mandarinoriental.com/landmark

9
The Woods, Central
Underground service

It's easy to miss this popular subterranean bar entered via a discreet door on Central's Hollywood Road. Owned by the three Chow sisters, The Woods serves cocktails designed with commendable attention to detail. All the ingredients are seasonal and the selection changes regularly.

Staple drinks include a Beet negroni made with beetroot-infused gin and a four-pepper margarita featuring jalapeño-infused tequila; during winter, cocktails based on flavours such as chestnuts, purple yams and brussels sprouts are served. The bar's lounge serves cocktails and offers a snack menu with simple dishes such as bruschetta. In the eight-seater Prix Fixe bar, cocktails are paired with complementary food.
LG, 17 Hollywood Road
+852 2522 0281
thewoods.hk

⑩

La Cabane Bistro, Central
C'est chic

Hong Kong is not short of French restaurants but there's perhaps nowhere more charmingly Gallic than La Cabane, a small and inviting wine bar found on Hollywood Road.

Specialising in biodynamic wine from around France, La Cabane's friendly team can expertly guide you through delicious wines from lesser-known, often independent vineyards. The space is casual and tight so best enjoyed with a small group. Oysters, cheeses, charcuteries and larger dishes can also be ordered.

62 Hollywood Road
+852 2776 6070
lacabane.hk

Retail
— A market economy

Every year around 50 million people flock to Hong Kong to shop their way around the city. It's not just the absence of retail tax that draws in the crowds: from luxury shopping centres to street markets, retail options abound at every price point.

Despite this, it's not easy to find high-quality homegrown brands in Hong Kong. With much of the city's clothing manufacturing having moved to the mainland over the past few decades, most keen shoppers are spending their cash on luxury brands from Europe and the US or cutting-edge labels from Japan and South Korea.

Our selection focuses on a mix of shopkeepers shaping independent retail and great examples of bricks-and-mortar shops from international brands. From family-run tailors to vintage-denim fanatics, read on to discover the best places to pick up something truly special.

Concept stores
Mixed retail

①
Kapok, Wan Chai
Future classics

When Frenchman Arnault Castel decided to open a mixed-retail space in 2006 he called it Kapok after a native tree known for its shady crown. He says, "We are a unique roof under which people can meet and find inspiring quality goods." After four years he transplanted Kapok to two separate shops in the Star Street precinct.

The St Francis Yard outpost focuses on fashion including homegrown womenswear label Berayah and shoes by Common Projects, while the Sun Street location stocks up on homeware such as trays by Hay from Denmark. Together with sister outlets at the PMQ design complex and K11 Art Mall, Castel hopes Kapok's emphasis on well-designed products will be "the antidote to shopping-mall boredom". It's a must-visit retail original.
5 St Francis Yard and 3 Sun Street
ka-pok.com

2

Undercover, Chai Wan
Out of this world

Stepping into the Undercover menswear shop in Chai Wan feels like entering another world thanks to the 2,000 lightbulb installation hanging overhead, cool concrete walls and a painting by 16th-century Flemish painter Joachim Patinir that spans almost the full width of the shop. Open since 2013, this is Japanese designer Jun Takahashi's footprint in Hong Kong. He founded the urban-chic Undercover streetwear label in 1993, which has since developed a reputation for sophistication and refinement while enthusiastically embracing bold punk elements.

"This shop is a more minimal and clean compared to previous designs," says Takahashi. Besides Undercover, the shop also stocks other Japanese brands, including White Mountaineering, Porter and Takahiromiyashita The Soloist.
Room 1709-1712, Block B, 18 Ka Yip Street
undercoverism.com

3

IT Hysan One, Causeway Bay
Global luxury brands

The distinctive black mortar edifice anchored at the intersection of Hysan Avenue, Leighton Road and Percival Street since 2011 is fashion multibrand retailer IT's flagship department store. Designed by Masamichi Katayama of Wonderwall, each of the four floors features a specific theme. The basement's industrial atmosphere targets men while the ground floor showcases house brands. On the first floor there is a casual environment appropriate for streetwear and the top floor is an elegant gallery setting befitting the luxury brands on show.

With hundreds of names from all over the world on display, the discerning shopper will recognise the likes of Comme des Garçons, Acne Studios and Maison Kitsuné. Yet they might also thrill at the discovery of a lesser-known brand of impeccable quality.
1 Hysan Avenue
ithk.com

4

GOD, Central
Spiritual experience

The name Goods Of Desire – or GOD for short – reflects the pride architects Douglas Young and Benjamin Lau have in their home city. The duo launched their brand selling homeware, stationery and accessories using Hong Kong motifs. It's impossible to mistake the metal letterboxes and iconic neon lights that adorn the brand's series of totes, wash bags and umbrellas. Today, GOD has six shops scattered across Hong Kong, including one on Hollywood Road that offers souvenir ideas across two floors.
48 Hollywood Road
+852 2805 1876
god.com.hk

Now, where is that lantern shop?

⑤
Joyce, citywide
Doyenne of designers

Since founder Joyce Ma opened her boutique at the Mandarin Oriental Hotel, Joyce has become an institution for the city's fashion-conscious residents. It was within its walls that Giorgio Armani and Prada, as well as avant-garde labels such as Dries Van Noten and Yohji Yamamoto, were introduced to Hong Kong.

The owner has since expanded into cosmetics with Joyce Beauty and Joyce Grooming stores. In 2014 Joyce Cares launched at Central's PMQ complex to give emerging designers a platform to sell their products. Today there are three Joyce boutiques across the city as well as locations in mainland China and Taiwan.
joyce.com

Business base
—
Our Hong Kong bureau is at the back of the shop

❻
Woaw, Central
Everything under the sun

Since its beginnings as an eyewear pop-up shop, Woaw has become one of the city's best concept stores. Stocking everything from tech accessories designed by Hong Kong's Native Union to toiletries from Malin + Goetz and Karen Walker sunglasses, it's a great place to explore. An acronym for World of Amazing Wonders, the spacious two-storey space also has a coffee shop called Elephant Grounds. Do some shopping after grabbing a coffee on the small balcony at the back; the ice-cream sandwiches, available at weekends only.
11 Gough Street
+852 2253 1313
woawstore.com

⑦
The Monocle Shop, Wan Chai
Work and play

On the corner of St Francis Yard, just off Queen's Road, our home in Hong Kong was the first of the comfy shop-cum-bureau formats that we have since replicated in Toronto, Tokyo and Singapore. Drop by to pick up the latest issue or to catch a glimpse of our team filing their reports to London. It's also a great place to buy gifts for your loved ones. The shop is stocked with our full range of collaborations, including signature Hinoki, Laurel and Sugi fragrances by Commes des Garçons and Porter carry-on bags.
1 St Francis Yard
+852 2804 2323
monocle.com

How am I going to fly home with this?

Department store
Shoppers' paradise

01 Lane Crawford, citywide
Urban cool

A Hong Kong icon with more than 160 years of history, Lane Crawford has evolved from a shop that traded in provisions for visiting ships' crews to become Greater China's largest luxury department store group.

Known for its discerning blend of established and upcoming designers, Lane Crawford offers brands exclusive to its Hong Kong locations. Gowns by Jason Wu, knitwear from Drumohr and linens from Frette are just a few of the labels only found at its own storefronts. Unlike many other luxury retailers of its kind there are no branded shop-in-shops at Lane Crawford; everything is pulled together to create a distinctive and memorable shopping experience for customers.

In 2014, Lane Crawford expanded its presence in Hong Kong with the opening of a new furniture and home-accessories store at the IFC mall. Designed by Yabu Pushelberg, the space mimics a large apartment featuring the best in interior design. Found on the fourth floor (the store overlooks Victoria Harbour, providing shoppers with spectacular views of the city's skyline), the shop stocks more than 155 brands, such as The Case Factory, Frette and The Rug Company.

Lane Crawford currently has five locations, including a home store and showroom at One Island South, two home stores in Admiralty and Central and two outlets in Causeway Bay and Tsim Sha Tsui.
lanecrawford.com

Home and interiors
Inspirational design

① Amelie & Tulips, Sheung Wan
Lessons in design

Amelie & Tulips in the Tai Ping Shan neighbourhood is a design retailer that was set up by Sappho Ma and Ellen Lai in 2012. The comfy interiors, informed by Scandinavian and Italian sensibilities, are flushed with natural light. Everything showcased here is impeccably presented to educate customers on how to furnish their own living spaces.

"We have smaller homes in Hong Kong," says Ma. "It's important that we show people how Scandinavian furniture is perfect for these environments."
56 Sai Street
+852 2291 0005
amelieandtulips.com

②
Casa Capriz, Wong Chuk Hang
Italian inspiration

Tucked away in one of Wong Chuk Hang's industrial buildings is one of the city's finest vintage furniture showrooms, Casa Capriz, set up by Italian Irene Capriz in 2012.

"It's a reflection of my background in fashion and eclectic personal style, as well as my love for bygone eras," says Capriz. Her stock (including desks, sofas and glassware) dates from the 1940s to the 1970s. Covering 240 sq m, it's the perfect place to find rare gifts such as a 1970s dining table by Angelo Mangiarotti.
16 Shui Ki Industrial Building,
18 Wong Chuk Hang Road
+852 9318 1730
casacapriz.com

③
General Store, Sheung Wan
Old and new

An eclectic pick of classic and modern-day interior goods lies waiting for visitors behind the heavy-metal green door of General Store, established in 2011 by Masayuki Fukada from Japan and American Shelly Hayashi. The white cube of a shop specialises in vintage-style paraphernalia such as its series of Edison bulbs and Deborah Bowness wallpaper, although contemporary iron vases from the US stand on the retail floor just as comfortably.

"We always try to have a variety of interesting and curious objects from different eras and parts of the world – there is no determining factor except that the design must last," says Hayashi. "The way we curate is to showcase the products and display items in an appealing and unexpected way."
41 Gage Street
+852 2851 8144
generalstoreltd.com

House to home
—
Archetypal's home is a restored shophouse

④
Archetypal, Wan Chai
Global design

This two-storey furniture and lighting shop was set up in 2013 by Desmond Wong. Instead of selling Scandinavian and Italian pieces like some rivals, Archetypal brings in unexpected homeware from other parts of the world. "We showcase innovations in material usage, craftsmanship and manufacturing processes, demonstrating how their beauty can merge seamlessly into our daily life," says Wong.

Products include the ceramic Bing ceiling lights by Resident and the elegant Outdoor Table Two from the UK's Another Country.
15 Moon Street
+852 2320 0580
archetypal.hk

Desmond Wong's top picks

01 **Chamber light by Lee:** Subtle light through translucent marble.
02 **Dwell lounge chair by Blu Dot:** Designed by Ralph Rapson and suitable for outdoor use.
03 **Dub light by EOQ:** Features metal sculpted into soft forms.
04 **Pick Up Sticks chair by Resident:** Solid oak frame with refined details.
05 **New Flutter range by Loveramics:** Inspired by classic Chinese flower-and-bird paintings.

5
Deem, Sheung Wan
Inviting design

Located along Hollywood Road is Deem, a furniture boutique that also serves as an art space for designers. Founded by designer Debra Little (*pictured*), Deem sells house-brand products inspired by mid-century modernism. Ranging from chairs and lighting to custom-made teapots, Deem's ethos is exemplified by the paintings and sculptures displayed in the shop. "We hope to show our customers how interior spaces can be curated to create inviting and enduring environments," says Little.
252 Hollywood Road
+852 2540 2011
deemlimited.com

Perfect picks

01 Void cast-brass bookends from Deem Made
02 Belgian tapered candles
03 Ceramics from Jars Collection
04 Enamel-and-silver spoons from David Andersen
05 Camel-hair throws from Rajasthan

⑥
Lala Curio, Wan Chai
Homely charms

Hailing from a family of craftsmen, interior designer Laura Cheung launched furniture and home-decor brand Lala Curio with the aim of resurrecting forgotten traditions and designs. The brand's lavishly decorated flagship space in Wan Chai's Sau Wa Fong neighbourhood is designed to replicate an actual home that has been generously filled with curios. With everything from sleek marble coffee tables to eye-catching colour-blocked lacquer boxes, home-interior enthusiasts are sure to lose track of time here.
32-33 Sau Wa Fong
+852 2528 5007
lalacurio.com

Quirky curios
Lala is the perfect place to pick up gifts

If I buy anything here I'll hang it off my tail

⑦

Manks, Wong Chuk Hang

Simple life

Ardent design-and-antique collectors Paul Fung and Susan Man injected the city with a dose of Scandinavian modernism when they set up Manks in 1996. The warehouse on Yip Fat Street sells mid-century chairs, sofas and other handpicked items of furniture.

"We are promoting a way of life where beauty and simplicity are married to function," says Fung, who represents design brands such as Fritz Hansen and Louis Poulsen. The shop also features a more compact range of homeware and decorative objects.

3F, 1 Yip Fat Street
+852 2522 2115
manks.com

⑧

K11 Design Store, Tsim Sha Tsui

Products to inspire

Occupying four units on K11 Art Mall's first floor, the K11 Design Store is the work of businessman Adrian Cheng. Set up in 2011, it features more than 1,000 products that are examples of original designs from Hong Kong and beyond. Whether it's cheery kitchenware from Italy's Alessi, a rugged yet sleek Côte&Ciel knapsack from France or speakers from homegrown Native Union, these products provide inspiration for making life that little bit better with some extra thought.

Shops 105, 110 and 111, K11 Art Mall, 18 Hanoi Road
+852 3110 5812
k11designstore.com

⑨

Igloo Homeware, Wan Chai

Small worlds

After working in the advertising industry for two decades, Dennis Chan and Nigel Keung decided it was time for a change. Drawing from their expertise building sets for commercials, the duo made a jump into the furniture business by opening Igloo Homeware. Many Hong Kong apartments lack space so Chan and Keung consciously selected a range of products that would suit smaller homes.

The shop's minimalist aesthetic is reflected in the wood furnishings and fixtures on sale. Beautifully crafted pieces made from solid oak and walnut imported from Japan sit alongside modern Scandinavian-designed lamps in the well-lit space. As well as furniture, smaller items such as cookware, decorations and tableware are available.

GF, 26 Sau Wa Court
+852 2520 0580
igloohk.com

Menswear
Bespoke and casualwear

①
Delstore, Wan Chai
Easy does it

Established in 2011, Delstore's two-storey outpost tucked away on Wan Chai's Schooner Street has been building a reputation for stocking quality men's and womenswear labels. The simple space reflects owners Derrick Leung and Ewing Cheng's penchant for an understated and elegant aesthetic. As well as Japanese brands such as Arts & Science and Italy's Barena, customers can take time to leaf through issues of independent periodicals including *Gather* and *Casa Brutus*. A sister store catering to female shoppers is around the corner. "We wanted shopping to be a slow-down experience," says Leung. Delstore certainly offers a pace of retail that is a happy contrast to Hong Kong's glitzy super labels.
3 Schooner Street
+852 2528 1770
delstore.co

②
Take5 Denim, Tsim Sha Tsui
Handy outpost

Take5 founder Benny Seki has been a fierce advocate of Amekaji – American-Japanese casual fashion – since 2000. Back then he began importing Japanese denim brands Evisu, Dry Bones, Gardener and Stormy Blue into Hong Kong, then persuaded them to collaborate on a denim called Take5.

It took some time for the market to warm to quality Japanese fashion but today Take5 has established itself as Asia's leading retailer of the best denim Japan has to offer. Customers can also peruse its wide range of leather accessories.
1F, 17 Cameron Road
+852 2375 5731
take5jeans.com

③
Juice, Sheung Wan
Fresh fashion top-ups

Paris's Bleu de Paname, London's A Sauvage, New York's Patrik Ervell and Copenhagen's Libertine-Libertine: if you're looking for great menswear brands you'll want to visit the Juice on Tai Ping Shan Street. "We opened this shop for customers looking for something edgy and premium," says co-founder Kevin Poon.

Close relationships with Nike and Adidas mean Poon and his buyers are able to get their hands on some of the world's most hard-to-find footwear. "As streetwear starts to mix into high fashion, we're at the melting pot between these two worlds."
18A-B Tai Ping Shan Street
+852 2517 3099

④
J.Crew, Central
Born in the USA

This icon of American fashion has been making headway in Hong Kong in recent years. J.Crew's first male-focused shop in Asia opened in Central's On Lan Street in 2014. The three-storey outpost's woody interiors feature J.Crew staples such as Ludlow suits and well-tailored chinos. Billing itself as a men's speciality shop, it's the place to go to check out the latest designs fresh off the New York catwalks, as well as exclusive collaborations with companies such as New Balance and Drakes. There's even a tailor on hand to help with the perfect fit.
9 On Lan Street
jcrew.com

⑤
Berluti, Central
Legacy leather

The luscious honey-hued exterior of the Berluti flagship at the base of Landmark Prince's building befits the rich legacy of this fourth-generation shoe-and-leather-goods company from Paris. Founded in 1895 by Alessandro Berluti, the firm has cemented a reputation over more than a century for impeccable workmanship and leather of extraordinary quality and elegance.

The supple materials used to make its bespoke and ready-to-wear shoes evolve and mature gracefully with age, developing a patina that imbues each pair with individuality. Customers at Landmark Prince's enjoy the best of old-school luxury, such as personalised monogram options and a patina service to bring out the shoes' best shade.
Store G21-G22 and M7-M8, Landmark Prince's
+852 2343 0855
berluti.com

Can someone give me a wing – I mean hand – with this thing?

⑥
The Armoury, Central
Design without borders

"We call our look 'international classic' because we take the best from different parts of the world," says Mark Cho at The Armoury (*see essay on page 82*). The Malaysian-born former property analyst founded his menswear retailer with Hong Kong native Alan See in 2010, converting a derelict third-floor unit of the Pedder Building into a cosy library of suits and shirts. Alongside its house-developed products, everything else on the racks and mannequins comes from small ateliers from around the world.

"We avoid designers who do not make their own products," says Cho. Customers can use the tailors, cordwainers and other artisans flown in especially to take orders. There is also a larger ready-to-wear shop in the Landmark.
307 Pedder Building,
12 Pedder Street
+852 2804 6991
thearmoury.com

⑦
FIL, Wan Chai
Get your fill

Hiroki Nakamura, the man behind Japanese streetwear brand Visvim, has two FIL shops in Hong Kong. We prefer the quieter cousin on Sun Street, footsteps away from our own bureau. Opened in 2011, the L-shaped shop's whitewashed brick interiors make for a calm shopping atmosphere that is rare in this bustling city.

The brand is well known for bringing traditional techniques into the 21st century, applying Japanese indigo kimono dyeing, for instance, to denim jackets. The firm takes care to ensure its merchandise gets the attention it deserves: the clothes are hung according to colour, while pairs of shoes such as Visvim's iconic FBT (a contemporary take on moccasins that features a rubber outsole suited to the city's concrete pavements) sit in neat rows.
8-9 Sun Street
+852 2528 3880
visvim.tv

❽
WW Chan, Central
Bespoke tradition

Back in the early 20th century a band of clothiers in Shanghai called the Red Gang borrowed the best of Russian, British, American, Japanese and Chinese techniques to develop a distinct brand of bespoke tailoring for gentlemen (*see essay on page 82*).

WW Chan, established in 1952, is one of the few remaining firms able to boast this lineage and has its main outlet in the Entertainment Building.

The bales of fabric in the shop's cabinets are sourced globally from mills such as Acorn in the UK. Each shirt features French seams with 22 stitches per inch, and the majority of the manufacturing process is done by hand. "To this day the only machine you will find at WW Chan is a straight sewing machine," says owner Peter Chan.
Unit B, 8F, Entertainment Building,
30 Queen's Road
+852 2366 9738
wwchan.com

❾
Ascot Chang, citywide
Measure for measure

In 1953 a Shanghai-trained shirtmaker named Ascot Chang established his first shop on Kimberley Road to cater to the rising demand for bespoke shirts cut from luxurious cloths. Today Ascot's son Tony (*pictured, second from right*) runs the company with Justin, the founder's grandson (*far right*). The brand's clientele reaches far and wide, including the likes of former US president George HW Bush, musician James Taylor and many of Hong Kong's most well-heeled businessmen.

Customers can choose from a range of 15 collars, four cuffs and eight monogram styles for their Oxfords at any of four shops (at the IFC Mall, Prince's Building, Elements shopping centre and The Peninsula). Once measured up you can order your Ascot Chang shirt from anywhere in the world. The brand also has stores in the US.
Citywide
ascotchang.com

Womenswear
Dressed to impress

①
Liger, Causeway Bay
Funky sophistication

If you're in the market for a pop of colour, interesting cuts and young brands from around the world, head to Liger: one of Hong Kong's most popular and fashion-forward women's boutiques. Actress Hilary Tsui and fashion buyer Dorothy Hui combined forces in 2009; together the duo scours the globe for unique and emerging brands and then bring them back for the local market. "Our style is funky yet sophisticated," says Hui of selecting which brands to carry.

The flagship shop on Paterson Street in Causeway Bay opened in 2013, welcoming visitors into a bright and spritely boutique that holds collections from the UK's Paper London, Pushbutton from South Korea and Austria's Petar Petrov. The pair have also come up with their own fashion label Oh My God, whose frocks frequently sport bold geometric silhouettes and vibrant colours.
Shop A&C Vienna Mansion,
55 Paterson Street
ligerstore.com

❷
Tikka, Central
Home and away

From its two-storey shop on Soho's Gough Street, Tikka has been surprising local shoppers and visiting tourists alike with emerging designers from Hong Kong and around the world since 2012. Homegrown fashion designer Doris Q's edgy and modern tops and skirts can be found hanging on the clothes racks alongside dresses from Paris's Damir Doma.

Shoppers wanting to complete their looks can also treat themselves to an eclectic selection of accessories, including clutches by Loeffler Randall from the US.
18 Gough Street
+852 2884 1111
tikka-boutique.com

③
Edit, Central
Everyday edit

Multibrand womenswear retailer Edit was established in 2011 by local architect Jacqueline Chak and Malaysian chartered accountant Genevieve Chew on Hollywood Road. Among the brands hanging on the railings are the UK's Studio Nicholson, Italian womenswear label Cote and Jacquemus from France. There is also a great accessories selection with jewellery from Vita Fede, shoes from Bionda Castana and bags by Sophie Hulme.

The duo have since rolled out their own in-house label, with the inaugural collection consisting of dresses and skirts that sport androgynous cuts and silhouettes that are meant for everyday living. "After running a store for a little bit more than two years we saw a little gap in the market for wearable yet fashionable and affordable clothing," says Chew.
67 Hollywood Road
+852 2549 4999
67edit.com

❹
ABoutique, Central
Custom-made collections

Hong Kong art director Andrew Cheng and product designer Jeannie Wong set up this multibrand womenswear shop in Soho in 2011, purverying their favourite finds from shopping trips in Europe and elsewhere. Shoppers can browse the collections of designers such as Orla Kiely from Ireland or Belgium's Essentiel Antwerp. "We do not follow current trends; everything you see here is in Jeannie's personal wardrobe," says Cheng from his shop, which sports a minimalist blue façade and clean modern interiors.
19 Aberdeen Street
+852 2851 6055
aboutique.hk

⑤
Russell Street, Central and Wan Chai
Quiet sophistication

Founded in 2011 by fashion professionals, Russell Street was set up across from Times Square but soon moved to locations in Wan Chai and Soho to sell women's fashion. The owners, who prefer anonymity to let their offerings speak for themselves, bring in fresh international brands every season, looking for clothes that are "special yet wearable". Besides launching Victoria Beckham's denim line, the shop introduced blouses and skirts by LA's Clover Canyon.
10C Aberdeen Street and
6 St Francis Yard
russell-street.com

⑥
Vein, Causeway Bay
Understated elegance

Inspired by the minimalist sensibility of the Scandinavian aesthetic, designer Melinda Wong (*pictured*) launched womenswear retailer Vein on Star Street in 2011, introducing Hong Kong to fashion brands from Sweden, Denmark and Finland. 2014 saw a move into bigger premises at Lee Gardens One. Separately, Vein's sister outpost on St Francis Yard sits right next to our own shop and offers fashion, accessories and homeware from more than 20 Nordic brands, such as Filippa K, Skultuna and Hay.

"We're presenting a new form of luxury, not only in a material sense but as it relates to qualities of grace, taste and peace of mind," says Wong. She's not just referring to the products for sale: the shop's clean interior design and white tiled walls echo her penchant for understated elegance.

Lee Gardens One, 33 Hysan Avenue
+852 2528 4988
bvein.com

7

Shanghai Tang, Central
Stately visions

It's not an understatement when Shanghai Tang calls its flagship location on Duddell Street a "mansion". Opened in 2012, this four-storey retailer – known for its modern take on traditional Chinese garment the *cheongsam* – boasts nearly 1,400 sq m of space, the largest of its stores in the world. Shanghai-based Design MVW drew from the Chinese art deco movement for the look and feel of the ornate interiors. There are two floors dedicated to womenswear, with separate sections for men, children, fragrances and homeware.
1 Duddell Street
+852 2525 7333
shanghaitang.com

Accessories and specialist retailers
The cherry on top

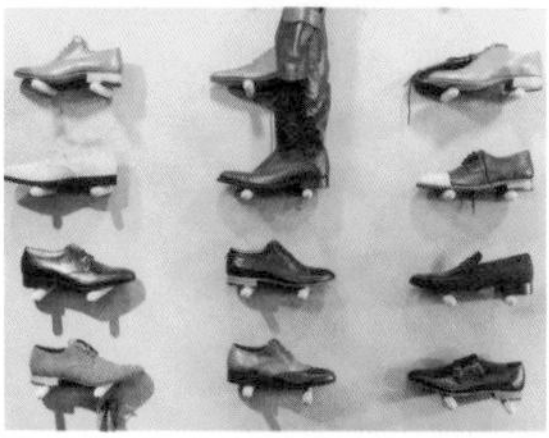

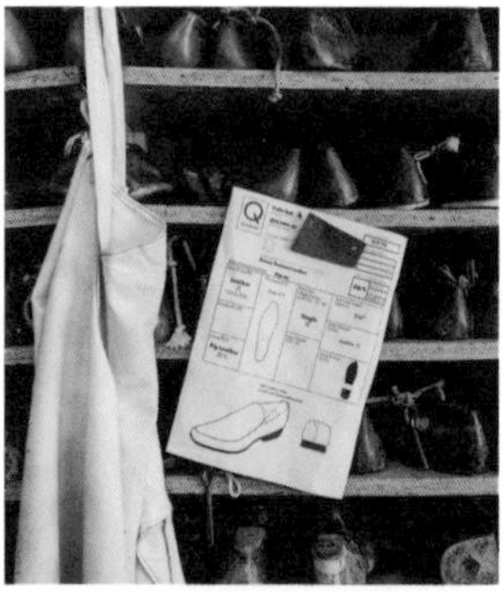

1

Shoe Artistry, Mong Kok
Keeping craft alive

Armed with the conviction that craftsmanship was worth saving, Jeff Wan and Kit Lee bought a 40-year-old bespoke shoe business and rebranded it as Shoe Artistry in 2012. "You can smell the leathers and hear hand tools and machines as we make our shoes," says Wan. Its two-storey retail and workspace on Tung Choi Street is a bustle of activity. Customers can browse the stock downstairs or attend classes upstairs on how to fashion leather footwear from raw materials. "We're exploring traditional craft in an urban context," adds Lee.
61 Tung Choi Street
+852 2796 6018
shoeartistry.info

Oh, there's more – I'm getting the rest delivered

②
Fungus Workshop, Sheung Wan
Joint effort

Fungus Workshop's unassuming and intimate space nestled in the artsy Po Hing Fong neighbourhood is a collaborative venture initiated in 2009 by leather designers and creatives Hoiming Fung, Baldwin Pui, Philip Lau and Grace Kwok. The boutique sells handmade leather products including wallets and rucksacks. For those who don't mind rolling up their sleeves, the owners conduct workshops on how to make accessories such as card-holders, coin pouches and camera bags.
4 Po Hing Fong
+852 2779 9003
fungusworkshop.net

③
Pye, Central and Admiralty
Ethical fashion

Shirting firm Pye traces its roots back to 1978, when YL Yang established a company that would have a strong social ethos at its core. Today it has a shop at the Central Building and one at Pacific Place. Run by granddaughter Dee Poon, it still focuses on ethical and sustainable production and the firm invests in every aspect of the process, from the growing of all its own cotton fabrics in Xinjiang to perfecting the shanks of each button. Even its packaging is based on the unique art of Chinese paper-folding.

Shirts here, which are made using Asian sizing, range from casual to formal and they are available in three different fits: lean, tailored and regular. If you're lucky enough to have flown first class with Cathay Pacific, you may have worn Pye's pyjamas on board.
Shops 19 and 22, Central Building and Shop 111, Pacific Place
pye.com.hk

④
Tai Ping Carpets, Kwai Chung
Quality underfoot

Tai Ping Carpets dates back to 1956, when it was founded by enterprising friends in Hong Kong. Since then its products have been sold across the globe, from private residences to hotels and even Buckingham Palace. At its flagship showroom on Kwai Cheong Road, the firm offers a range of ready-made rugs, including the Japanese-inspired Yukata design from the shop's Haiku Collection and the misty grey Lagune from the Etats d'âme Collection. Custom rugs are also available.
8F, Tower 1, Kowloon Commerce Centre, 51-53 Kwai Cheong Road
+852 2848 7668
Taipingcarpets.com

5

Tassels, Central

Footwear to impress

In 2000 a management consultant, accountant, investment banker and IT executive got together to found dress-shoe retailer Tassels. "We realised choices back then were very limited, then one of us went to Tokyo and bought a comfy pair of Aldens – Tassels was born from there," says co-founder Victor Kwan. The team started with a series of pop-ups to introduce the brand before launching their first standalone in 2006.

Housed in the basement of the Landmark shopping centre, the shop showcases a variety of brands that include Aldens, Edward Green and Bontoni. "All the brands we carry are family businesses with an extended history," says Kwan. Meanwhile, those in need of a quick fix can use the in-house shoe-shine service.

Shop B64-65, Basement, Landmark shopping centre
+852 2789 9911
tassels.com.hk

6

Loveramics, Causeway Bay

Tableware with an edge

Loveramics – a portmanteau of "love" and "ceramics" – is an urban loft-style china-tableware shop set up just off Leighton Road in 2009. William Lee founded the company with his wife Grace Ching and the couple take pride in the timelessness of the products they design and sell, both in terms of style and quality.

"Our products have a bit of contemporary style and are slightly edgy; they may not be the most easy to love but are absolutely functional," says Lee. He is alluding to the firm's eclectic range of designs, from a pared-down minimalist teapot set to a more colourful and abstract collection of plates.

While most proud of its own products, Loveramics also carries a selection of porcelain merchandise from around the world.

GF, 97 Leighton Road
+852 2915 8018
loveramics.com

7

The Bottle Shop, Sai Kung

First-rate tipple

Tracy Gan and Danny Wong (*both pictured, top*) set up their bricks-and-mortar beer shop in 2012, stocking craft brews, wines and spirits that cannot be easily found in the typical Hong Kong corner shop. "We decided to import a few items we knew were of very high quality and make them available to the public," says Wong.

Top picks include Australia's Hop Hog or a cherry-and-raspberry beer by Bacchus from Belgium. Thanks to the city's liberal alcohol laws it's perfectly OK to grab a bottle here and head to the nearby Sai Kung harbour to take in the sunset.

114 Man Nin Street
thebottleshop.hk

Bookshops
Top reads

1 Kubrick, Yau Ma Tei
Between the covers

Housed inside the beloved arthouse cinema Broadway Cinematheque in Yau Ma Tei, Kubrick is not your typical bookshop. In fact it doubles as a café, recordshop and gallery, where works by artists are for sale. Lectures, talks and workshops with writers and film-makers are regularly hosted in-store.

English, Chinese and foreign-language books, ranging from novels to self-help manuals, are available alongside more obscure titles. The shop stocks a variety of CDs and DVDs and there is even a collection of vinyl tucked away; weary customers can drop by the café for a caffeine fix pre- or post-browse. A rare find in Hong Kong, Kubrick should feature on any cinephile or booklover's go-to checklist.
Shop H2, Cinema Block, Prosperous Garden, 3 Public Square
+852 2384 8929
kubrick.com.hk

Real page-turner — Caffeine and books combine in Kubrick

Four more

01 **Page One, Harbour City, Canton Road, Tsim Sha Tsui:** Bookshop chain Page One has its flagship location at the Harbour City building. Besides a catalogue of English and Chinese titles, customers can browse through a broad range of global periodicals. Once you have made up your mind, head to the in-store bakery to rest your legs and thumb through your latest purchase.
pageonegroup.com

02 **Eslite, Causeway Bay:** Taiwanese chain Eslite opened its first overseas outlet in Hong Kong's shopping district of Causeway Bay in 2012. The three-floor outpost's shelves are well stocked with English and Chinese-language books and magazines, plus titles from small independent publishers. There is also a corner of listening booths for music buffs.
eslite.com

03 **Kelly & Walsh, Admiralty, Central:** Among the city's top independent bookshops, Kelly & Walsh carries a mix of English-language fiction and non-fiction works, as well as a wide variety of special-interest books.
kellyandwalsh.com

04 **Bondi Books, Chai Wan:** Situated in an industrial building in Chai Wan, this is a treasure trove of exclusive first-edition books and prints. Among the rare titles on display is an Oscar Wilde-signed *Salome* from 1893. Customers have to make an appointment before visiting.
bondibooks.com

Street markets
Outdoor shopping

Well heeled
Be sure to wear comfy walking shoes

①

Best markets
Blue-sky retail

Even if you end up not buying anything, immersing yourself in the street markets of Kowloon is well worth the experience. A much grittier and more authentic affair compared to shopping in generic department stores, there is never a dull moment amid the colourful tarpaulin stalls that have become a symbol of old Hong Kong. Many specialise in specific products and if you want to buy something you should prepare for a verbal joust: haggling is common practice here.

If you have a full day spare, take the MTR to Prince Edward Station and work your way down south, using Nathan Road as your guide. Three blocks east from the station you will happen upon ❶ *Flower Market*, which leads on to ❷ *Yuen Po Street Bird Market*. Both are open daily from morning to sunset and some fresh flowers and birdsong are not a bad way to start the day. Then head south (remaining on the east side of Nathan Road) to ❸ *Fa Yuen Street Market*, which sells trainers from all the big brands including Nike, Adidas and New Balance. Cut west to the parallel ❹ *Tung Choi Street Fish Market*, where bags of goldfish and aquatic plants can be found hanging from the walls.

Continue on Tung Choi Street after Argyle Street, passing Mong Kok Station on the right. This is the ❺ *Ladies Market*, which traditionally catered to women but now carries a host of quirky souvenirs for all and sundry.

Further south, tackle the famous ❻ *Temple Street Night Market*. Open daily from 16.00 till midnight, this nocturnal bazaar, where everything from watches to luggage can be found, buzzes with tourists and locals alike. Even if you don't feel like shopping, it's still the perfect place to experience old Hong Kong at its best.

Contact details

01 **Flower Market:** *flower-market.hk*
02 **Yuen Po Street Bird Market:** *bird-garden.hk*
03 **Fa Yuen Street Market:** *sneakers-street.hk*
04 **Tung Choi Street Fish Market:** *goldfish-market.hk*
05 **Ladies Market:** *ladies-market.hk*
06 **Temple Street Night Market:** *temple-street-night-market.hk*

Things we'd buy

— Objects of desire

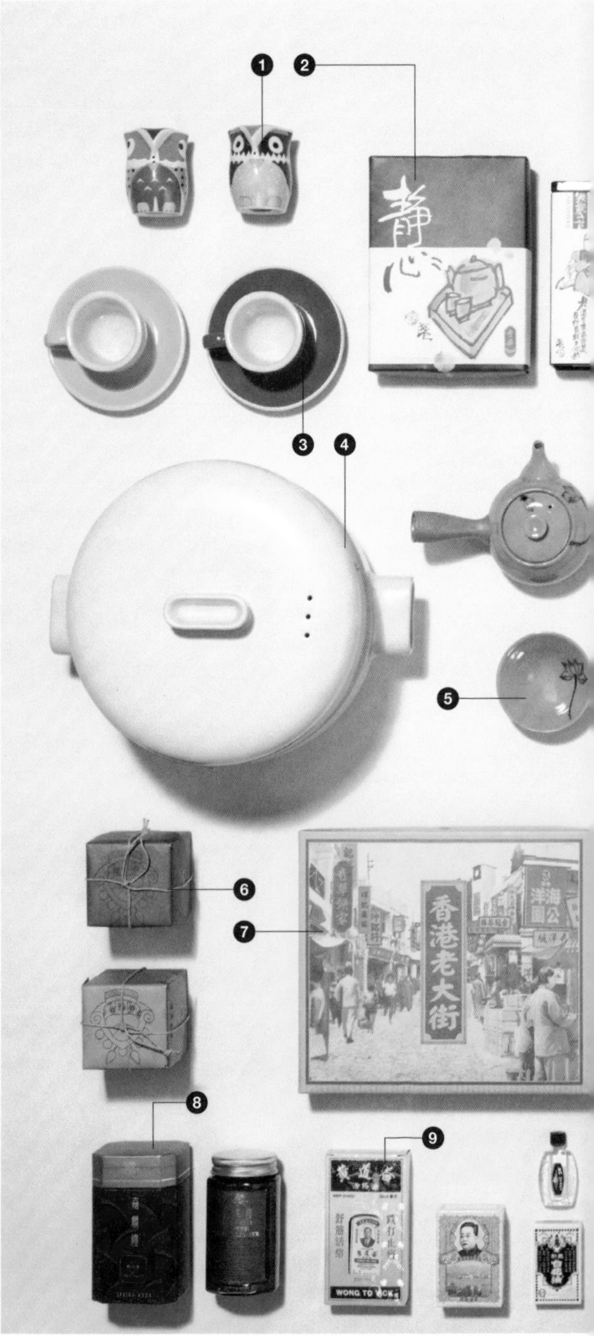

You'll find it hard to spend time in Hong Kong and not feel the urge to do some shopping. It's a place where global luxury brands seem to occupy every street corner and shopping malls are the hubs of their communities.

But browse beyond the international flagships to smaller scale bricks-and-mortar retail and you'll find some great things that are unique to Hong Kong and perfect for mementos or gifts. Be it delicate stone "chops" (stamps) sold from street-market stalls, watches designed and made in the city, traditional medicines or well-tailored shirts, there's much more to this city's retail than those designer shoes and handbags.

01 Owlets salt-and-pepper shakers by Top Choice *topchoice.com.hk*
02 Chinese tea by Kee Wah *keewah.com*
03 Cups and saucers by Loveramics *loveramics.com*
04 Ding steam cooker by Office for Product Design *officeforproductdesign.com*
05 Teaware by Lock Cha *lockcha.com*
06 Handmade clay by Soul Art Shop *+852 2857 7786*
07 Traditional box of snacks by Kee Wah *keewah.com*
08 XO chilli sauce by Spring Moon at Peninsula *peninsulaboutique.com*
09 Wong To Yick, Po Chai pills and white-flower oil *Available from chemists citywide*
10 Magnetic car toy and chalk sticks by Huzi Design *huzidesign.com*
11 Portable Chinese chequers from Cosmos Books *cosmosbooks.com.hk*
12 Table-tennis paddles by Huzi Design *huzidesign.com*
13 Brass candle holder by Deem *deemlimited.com*
14 Solid ink by Man Luen Choon *manluenchoon.com*
15 Chinese ink and calligraphy brush by Man Luen Choon *manluenchoon.com*
16 Stone 'chops' by Kingstone *+852 6146 8998*
17 Cantoon retro notebooks by Daycraft *daycraft.co*
18 Watch by Kitmen Keung *kitmenkeung.com*
19 Sunglasses from Smith & Norbu *smith-norbu.com*

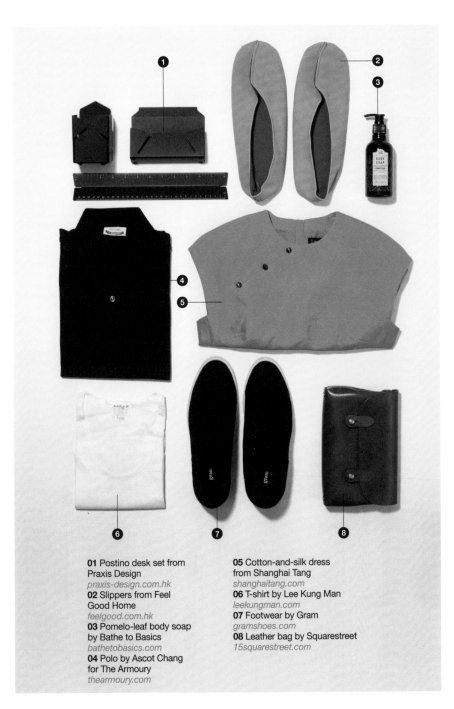

01 Postino desk set from Praxis Design
praxis-design.com.hk
02 Slippers from Feel Good Home
feelgood.com.hk
03 Pomelo-leaf body soap by Bathe to Basics
bathetobasics.com
04 Polo by Ascot Chang for The Armoury
thearmoury.com
05 Cotton-and-silk dress from Shanghai Tang
shanghaitang.com
06 T-shirt by Lee Kung Man
leekungman.com
07 Footwear by Gram
gramshoes.com
08 Leather bag by Squarestreet
15squarestreet.com

12 essays
— Hong Kong's hidden stories

So many stories to stick my beak into

ESSAY 01

Hollywood dreaming
Hong Kong's ancient soul

The story of Hollywood Road is the story of Hong Kong and its journey from empire to international hub for art and commerce. But its antique shops were also where one man set up a museum, one item at a time.

by Lynn Fung, museum director

All teenagers are self-centred and navel-gazing and nowhere is this more true than in Hong Kong. Well, in my experience anyway. When I was growing up in this tiny city there were only a handful of neighbourhoods that mattered to me. The Peak was where my house was located and my primary school was there, too. Admiralty housed the closest McDonald's to school while my dad's office was in Central. Causeway Bay was home to the Jockey Club and where mum made her trips to the market. Anything outside of those places I experienced in a blurry haze, if at all, existing only as a name on a map or something you drove through en route to somewhere else – ideally McDonald's.

One of these half-remembered places was Hollywood Road. My family and I had a dim-sum lunch every Saturday at the same restaurant for 26 years: Zen in Admiralty, which has since closed down. After these lunches my dad would ask us to drop him off on Hollywood Road and fetch him before dinner.

"Hollywood Road was the second road to be paved in the colony and it has served as an antiques mecca"

What were my first memories of that road? Firstly, that it was far. For teenage me, Central started at the old Furama Hotel at the beginning of Queen's Road Central and ended somewhere around the old Lane Crawford, 200 metres down the road (now home to a massive Zara flagship). Sheung Wan, Sai Yung Pun, Kennedy Town: all were unknown entities. Hollywood Road belongs to Sheung Wan proper and in those days it was all musty antique shops nestled between coffin shops (from which you averted your eyes lest you beguile some restless spirit who was waiting to come home with you). Man Mo Temple pumped out incense smoke and the reigning colour of the landscape was grey, speckled with the faded red and chipped gold of old shop signs.

Why did my father insist on taking his walkabouts there? I suspect that in the beginning it had something to do with his job in property development and the enjoyment he took from walking around Hong Kong to get a sense of what the next up-and-coming neighbourhood might be. He had already invested in Soho and I gathered he was venturing west to see what possibilities lay there. That might have been his original purpose but that wasn't what caused him to return week after week, year after year.

What really lured him back were the family-owned, generations-old antique shops. Hollywood Road used to be close

Fung's favourites

01 The Chairman, Central
Hands-down the best Cantonese in the city.

02 Serge et le Phoque, Wan Chai
Modern French in the heart of a dirty wet market.

03 Kishoku, Causeway Bay
The finest sushi and sashimi outside of Japan.

to the coastline 100 years ago. It was the second road to be paved in the colony and it has served as an antiques mecca since its inception. Europeans sailing back home often looked for Chinese knick-knacks and artefacts to buy for loved ones (or to show off their worldliness) and the ever-enterprising Chinese set up shop along this road to sate their demands.

In the 1980s, Hollywood Road saw a new influx of antiques. China had started to loosen its borders, resulting in large supplies of classical antique furniture from the Ming and Qing dynasties made of the precious (and now virtually extinct) hardwoods *huanghuali* and *zitan*. These were sold for a pittance as there was no market for them.

No market apart from my slightly eccentric father, who fell in love and continued his love affair for the next 40 years, gradually accumulating what is now one of the world's largest collections of these classical pieces. To my mother's despair he stored them in our house, replacing our regular furniture piece by piece until one day my sister woke up in a late-Ming six-poster bed.

Today the Hollywood Road area has a changed landscape. Among the remaining antique shops there are coffee houses, whisky bars, an Italian *enoteca*, a contemporary Russian art gallery, the prerequisite Aesop store and – right near my office – a bar decorated with works by Jeff Koons and, supposedly, Damien Hirst. Though technically still part of Sheung Wan, Hollywood Road has been gentrified to become the cooler, artsier and more authentic sister of Soho. You are as likely to hear French as Cantonese through the streams of Korean that is spoken by the legions of tourists, clutching their egg tarts from Tai Cheong Bakery while waiting their turn to take a selfie in the Man Mo Temple courtyard.

This dreamy, ill-defined part of my childhood landscape is now a permanent fixture of my adult life. My office is inside the Liang Yi Museum (located at 181-199 Hollywood Road), Hong Kong's largest private museum and a place founded by my father to house his collections. Befitting the neighbourhood, the museum's permanent collections include two types of antiques. The first are European vanity cases from the late 1880s to 1960s; all beautiful, bejewelled and highly technical precursors to our modern-day clutches and compacts.

The second? Well, my mother finally got her way: the antiques are out of our home so it's once again furnished with inconspicuously elegant modern pieces. Those Ming and Qing pieces – which were such an eyesore to her yet priceless on the open market – have finally found their permanent home on a newly chic Hollywood Road. — (M)

i

ABOUT THE WRITER: Prior to taking on the mantle of running her family's private museum, Lynn Fung was a food journalist and editor. She can usually be found trying out one of Hollywood Road's many trendy new restaurants, bemoaning the rapid gentrification of the neighbourhood over a pint of beer or glass of wine.

ESSAY 02

Director's cuts

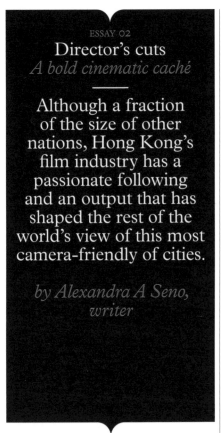

A bold cinematic caché

Although a fraction of the size of other nations, Hong Kong's film industry has a passionate following and an output that has shaped the rest of the world's view of this most camera-friendly of cities.

by Alexandra A Seno, writer

There's a scene – about 12 minutes into John Woo's *Hard Boiled* (1992) – where Alan, the suave killer played by Tony Leung Chiu-wai, careens through the streets of Hong Kong in a zippy top-down red convertible, an electro-jazz tune playing in the background. With the wind in his slick hair, sunshine on his face and wide-angle vistas of gleaming glass-and-steel skyscrapers and construction cranes before him, Alan looks like the epitome of a carefree urbanite. Except that he is actually on his way to commit a cold-blooded hit. The film only gets better from that point onwards and is an indication of why Woo's place in global cinema is undisputed.

Of all the art forms to have emerged out of Hong Kong, film holds pride of place. Like one of the everyman-turned-hero characters in the territory's movies, Hong Kong films have braved the odds through the decades to win audiences worldwide and receive accolades at festivals in Cannes, Berlin and many places besides. These films gave the world a glimpse of Hong Kong as it viewed itself and spun dreams of life in the city; the grit and the glamour of crusaders and survivors. Hong Kong basks in that ethereal neon glow.

After 1949, the time when the Communist party came to power in China, Hong Kong became a refuge for many of Shanghai's film veterans. That shifted the axis of Chinese entertainment to the territory. From the 1950s onwards, the Shaw Brothers and Cathay studios made movie musicals inspired by Chinese opera to the delight of the diaspora, which ranged from the progeny of tin-mine labourers in Malaysia to the exiles in Taiwan and the homesick in Chinatowns around the world.

In the 1960s and 1970s the industry created Hong Kong

Hong Kong films

01 **Hard Boiled (1992)**
John Woo's unrepentantly stylish shoot'em up.
02 **Infernal Affairs (2002)**
Cop thriller later remade by Martin Scorsese.
03 **Night and Fog (2009)**
Ann Hui's drama about the unravelling of the Hong Kong dream.

martial-arts films. In *Fists of Fury* (1972), Bruce Lee was already an international star. In it he worked with a young stuntman who a few years later would achieve fame as the legendary kung-fu comic Jackie Chan.

In the 1980s and 1990s, Hong Kong came into its own by projecting its rich-city swagger into cinema, be it with an action-comedy such as Eric Tsang Chi-wai's *Aces Go Places* (1982) or the lush imagery of Wong Kar Wai's *Days of Being Wild* (1990). Who can forget the piercing gaze of the eternally handsome leading man Andy Lau Tak-wah as a motorcycle racer in Derek Yee Tung-sing's *Full Throttle* (1995)?

In its heyday during those two decades, Hong Kong was making more than 200 films a year. But with a domestic audience of only seven million and shifting tastes in the once-voracious export markets of Southeast Asia, South Korea, Japan and Taiwan, it has since changed. Today it is considered a good year when 40 films are made in Hong Kong. Mainland China and its hundreds of millions of cinema-goers are now the mother lode of box-office gold and big production budgets. The vast majority of Hong Kong's acting and directing talent gets most of its work across the border now.

"The heart of Hong Kong cinema continues to beat to its own particular rhythm. Now and then a gem will appear, showcasing the city's potential"

However, the heart of Hong Kong cinema continues to beat to its own particular rhythm. Now and then a gem will appear, showcasing the city's potential for stories. From the depths of the industry's doldrums, Andrew Lau Wai-keung and Alan Mak Siu-fai's police thriller *Infernal Affairs* (2002) proved that Hong Kong still had what it takes to entertain the world. Martin Scorsese remade it as *The Departed* (2006), winning a best-film Oscar in the process.

Ann Hui On-wah's murder-drama *Night and Fog* (2009) revealed an unravelling of family life in the destitute Tin Shui Wai district, pushed up against a rising China. The prolific director Johnnie To Kei-fung has enthralled viewers with everything from *Yesterday Once More* (2004), about jewel thieves in love, to

Triad Election (2006), about succession in organised crime.

Everyone who has been seduced by Hong Kong films probably has a favourite cinematic memory of the city, imagined or real. It could be Maggie Cheung Man-yuk in her colourful 1960s *cheongsam* and big hair navigating the alleys of her apartment complex in *In the Mood for Love* (2000). Chow Yun-fat in his long black trench walking coolly through a construction site in *A Better Tomorrow* (1986). Daniel Wu in a blaze of camera flashes from a wall of Hong Kong's infamous paparazzi in *The Heavenly Kings* (2006).

We feel as if we've all been there. Hong Kong was just made for the movies. — (M)

i

ABOUT THE WRITER: Alexandra A Seno writes about visual art, design and film in Asia. She also serves on the executive committee of the Oriental Ceramic Society of Hong Kong, the advisory council of Spring Workshop and on the board of Para Site, Hong Kong's leading non-profit independent art organisation.

ESSAY 03

Breaking the mould
Members' clubs rule OK

Although difficult to procure, an invite to Hong Kong's Foreign Correspondents' Club provides a tantalising glimpse of the city's hospitality at its best. New enterprises, take note.

by Aisha Speirs, Monocle

If I'm going to be completely honest, putting together certain sections of this guide involved a bit of a gamble. As in most global cities, thousands of people arrive in Hong Kong every year with the dream of making something of themselves. The city's low barriers to entry for starting a business, great international links and relatively stable economy makes it an attractive place for entrepreneurs to set up shop. It's also a city where weekday lunches are an important affair and nearly anyone will assert that their favourite dim-sum place, *dai pai dong* (street-food stall) or *cha chaan teng* (tea place) is the best. Food is a big deal here. And so it's no surprise that restaurateurs from both Hong Kong and abroad see the city as fertile ground for a new venture.

But along with independent retail, cafés and restaurants in the city face stiff competition and high rents can put a rapid expiry date on their existence. While it can be disheartening to see the money and effort that goes into launching a new enterprise wasted, the frequently brief nature of doing business here does a lot to emphasise the special qualities of places that have managed to endure.

For me, this comfort is felt most deeply at the Foreign Correspondents' Club, or FCC. Located in an iconic brick building just above the fray of Central, it's neither the city's oldest nor most exclusive club. But the subtlety with which it exists sets it apart from the hundreds of more visible restaurants and bars that it has outlived.

Now, I understand that there's a certain cruelty to including a place that only members can visit on the pages of a travel guide. And while I hope that some of you have friends who can take you or that you can arrange reciprocal membership via clubs back home (visiting journalists can join temporarily while in town), the rules that are enforced there are part of what makes it special.

Unlike nearly every other bar or café in Hong Kong, you're not at risk of sitting near someone having a loud phone conversation or being notified of a stream of text messages. Here, phone calls are prohibited unless you are in the foyer or next to one of the club telephones. Cash is also not visible as tabs are payable on members' accounts, meaning that people tend to make friends and buy rounds for each other rather than having to get out the calculator to tally up a receipt.

Beneath the whirring fans of the club's main bar, journalists and photographers meet and share stories. You're liable to strike up a conversation with the likes of High Court judges or war correspondents. There are no gimmicks or games and if anyone throws a strop, they're not likely to be welcome back.

"The FCC is an unpretentious place that represents free speech, a free press and the free movement of people – all things facing challenges in Hong Kong"

At the heart of the place are the staff, some of whom have been around for decades. Their happiness is as important to the club as that of the members (a rare approach in Hong Kong's hierarchical social history), their assistance is attentive without being sycophantic and their dedication is in stark contrast to the often temporary nature of Hong Kong's service industry.

It may seem strange to dedicate this many words to one place in a city that is full of bars, restaurants and private clubs. But the FCC is somewhere that holds strong to standards that other parts of Hong Kong are letting slip. This isn't just about its rules regarding mobile phones and the treatment of staff. It's an unpretentious place that represents free speech, a free press and the free movement of people – all things facing challenges in Hong Kong. It's a place where time seems to stand still but where the future of the city is at the top of the agenda. It's never going to be the hottest table in town nor win any culinary awards but if someone offers to meet you here for a drink, you'd be a fool to say no. — (M)

Hong Kong books

01 Fragrant Harbour by John Lanchester
Charts the city's shifting identity.

02 Hong Kong Noir by Feng Chi-shun
Reveals the city's darker side.

03 Love in a Fallen City by Eileen Chang
Hazy and romantic short stories.

i

ABOUT THE WRITER: Aisha Speirs is a MONOCLE contributing editor and our former Hong Kong bureau chief. Raised in London, she left MONOCLE's New York bureau to work in Hong Kong for a year in 2013 and has never left.

ESSAY 04

Flight of fancy

Ode to an airport

Providing real substance to the notion of a transport hub, Hong Kong International Airport – the last hurrah of the outgoing British power – is a lesson in well-executed infrastructure projects and a joy to behold.

by Tristan McAllister, Monocle

As the 777 on which you've been seated for 16 hours starts to shudder and tilt to the right, you look out the window quickly in your groggy state to see the spoilers on the wing flip up. Your fast-moving jet is shedding speed in preparation for its final approach. Then a kind flight attendant leans into your seat and thanks you for flying that day – somehow she manages the 16 hours without so much as a hair out of place.

By the time the landing gear is deployed, your seat is fully upright and you've wrestled enough of your consciousness back to start thinking about where you are. Again looking out your window, you now see the haze of the South China Sea and the fast ferries that dot the water before you. From nowhere, tarmac. Lower, slower. Roll left. Roll right. Touch down.

Welcome to Hong Kong International Airport (HKIA). In many ways this hub seems to pay homage to British colonial rule. The airport was finished right about when the Queen handed the thriving economic city-state back to the Chinese. If you ask people in Hong Kong they'll tell you the airport was a bit of a capstone on British rule: a way to galvanise the city's strength as a regional hub and keep Hong Kong active in the international game. This in spite of the post-handover fears about what Beijing's reign might do to the place.

Whether fear that Hong Kong would slip back was warranted, HKIA is clearly a place where things move forward. It's placed itself squarely in the worldwide super-

HKIA hotspots

01 **The Wing Lounge**
Don't miss the noodles at Cathay Pacific's flagship lounge.

02 **Cinema**
Hong Kong's largest Imax theatre means a long layover never looked so good.

03 **Limousine Lounge**
The best way to avoid the kerbside confusion.

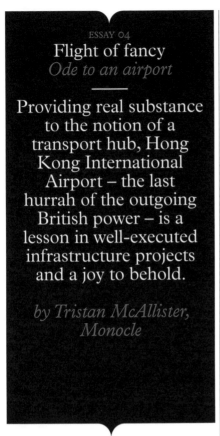

"This is one of the few places in the world where you can land and transit to a ferry without ever clearing customs"

hub game and as you disembark you begin to understand why.

More freight passes through the airport in a year than anywhere else in the world; its passenger numbers rank it in the top 10 internationally. Beyond the numbers it's one of the best airports at which any delay-stricken traveller could get stuck. An Imax theatre, eclectic food options and some of the world's best premium lounges mean that you could leave a prolonged stint at the airport in a better state than when you arrived (North America and Europe, pay attention).

HKIA is not just an airport: it's multimodal. Yes, I know the term is annoying but it's appropriate nonetheless. You can catch just about any other mode of transport from the airport. This is one of the few places in the world where you can land and transit to a ferry without ever clearing customs; the planners put a ferry terminal right at the edge of the airport. Travellers heading for points around the Pearl River Delta can walk right off their flights and onto a boat, going through customs for the Chinese mainland at their destination.

If staying in the Special Administrative Region of Hong Kong, opt for the Mass Transit Railway's fast train. It takes you straight from the airport to the city centre in 24 minutes, the carriages are clean, the views spectacular and the fare very affordable. Gargantuan spans of roadway and bridge slung from island to island make this archipelago navigable, running 35km from HKIA to the centre. The scale and attention to design are stunning.

Once in the city you realise how central these transport links are; even though Hong Kong's districts don't spread out too much the connectivity is impressive. And you'll likely notice these things throughout your stay as you ride the metro lines or wait at the Central Ferry Pier to step aboard a Star Ferry for a trip across Victoria Harbour.

While on the harbour, look east on the Kowloon side and try to see the sprawling terminal at Kai Tak Airport. Any passenger who had the chance to sit on a Cathay Pacific 747 during final approach to the city's former airport will say that you felt as though you were spying on the private lives of Hong Kongers in their homes who were just mere metres off the wing-tip. While privacy wasn't necessarily a reason to move the airport, Kai Tak was simply outgrown. I'm sure the neighbours are happy and so too are the cruise lines that now call at the airport-cum-seaport.

When you build a city on an island, infrastructure is critical to that city's success. What's inspiring about Hong Kong is the way in which the application of urban planning has evolved from old to new. The city has become known for it.

On your return journey through HKIA you'll notice that the airlines have actually put check-in counters at the MTR station in the city centre. You'll collect your boarding pass, drop your suitcase, peruse some of the adjoining shops and take a leisurely stroll onto the train without really having to think about what you're doing. At the airport and through security, you board your plane. You drop into your seat – once again it's a 777. You hope for a restful flight but mostly you wish that your next destination made it as easy and interesting as Hong Kong does. — (M)

ABOUT THE WRITER: Tristan McAllister is a contributing editor at MONOCLE and our former transport editor. Based in New York and regularly flying in and out of American airports, he knows what it's like to not have an efficient and comfortable airport like HKIA within easy reach.

ESSAY 05

Everything is illuminated

The city's neon obsession

The daily Symphony of Lights show on Victoria Harbour may make for a quirky visitor attraction but it also points to Hong Kong's longstanding love of bright lights.

by Aric Chen, design curator

Perhaps one of the odder things that visitors can check out in Hong Kong is the outdoor Symphony of Lights show. Starting at 20.00 daily, dozens of buildings on either side of Victoria Harbour light up with laser beams and crowns of spiralling searchlights. At designated locations you can supplement the experience with piped-in music and narration. Or you might not notice anything at all. Indeed, the Symphony of Lights is like an extra dollop of icing atop an already well-decorated cake; isn't Hong Kong lit up enough already?

But while LED screens (and lasers and searchlights) vie for attention, for most of its modern history Hong Kong's glow has come from its neon signs. Using the electrified gas-filled tubes perfected in the early 20th century by French chemist Georges Claude, neon signs first arrived in Hong Kong in about 1920. The medium took hold slowly at first but by 1964 a government report could exuberantly describe how "a million neon signs light the streets proclaiming their messages in every colour".

At the time, neon signs were a symbol of prosperity. A giant diamond announced the Precious Gem restaurant in Sham Shui Po. On Nathan Road, Millie's enticed shoppers with a three-storey-high burst of illuminated peacock feathers, while a crown-topped sceptre presided over the Chinese Palace Night Club. Guinness World Records declared National Panasonic's sign, also on Nathan Road, as the world's largest. In a city of vertiginous density, neon has dominated Hong Kong's cityscape and graphic lexicon at both extremes of vision.

In fact, neon became so synonymous with the city as to become completely inseparable from it. One could argue that Hong Kong in the popular imagination would be a lesser place if not for the films of Wong Kar-wai with their moody neon glow. According to the director's then-cinematographer, Christopher Doyle: "The films we made [in the] 1980s and 1990s wouldn't be this way if it wasn't for the space in which they were made. And our space is a neon space." In the days of tighter budgets, the film-makers were simply "stealing the neon light", he adds.

The hard-won romance of neon also infiltrated Hong Kong's other great cultural export: Cantopop music. In his 1987 hit "Love Each Other," Jacky Cheung croons: "Each and every light slowly fades away. The city's hustle and bustle finally quiets down. Neon lights glow in the dusk every day, resting on a hard day's night." That is to say the city, its people and neon have long been conflated, their rhythms thrumming in sync.

"In a city of vertiginous density, neon signs have dominated Hong Kong's cityscape and graphic lexicon at both extremes of vision"

However, neon signs are all but disappearing from Hong Kong's streets. While local government once boasted of their ubiquity, it's now nearly regulating them out of existence. But the main culprit is obsolescence: the pointillist lights of energy-efficient LED signage are quickly replacing neon's flickering lines.

Of course, visitors can still find stubborn concentrations of neon signs lighting the nightclubs of Wan Chai, the pawn shops and mahjong parlours of Yau Ma Tei and the restaurants and shopping emporia of Nathan Road. All the while, new neon signs are popping up in fashionable shops and restaurants, bent and twisted into retro designs. You could say that neon signs are becoming to LEDs what vinyl records are to digital recordings: a beloved, anachronistic relic.

So let's not get too sentimental. Technology is meant to become outdated and a city's job is to change. Perhaps one day we'll get weepy-eyed for LEDs, too. In the meantime you'll see plenty of them emblazoned across the buildings of the Symphony of Lights – except IM Pei's Bank of China building. Its 72 floors still light up in neon. — (M)

Best neon signs

01 Tsui Wah, Central
Each location for this chain of diners has a different sign.
02 Victory mahjong parlour, Yau Ma Tei
Spans the façade's entire width.
03 Sammy's Kitchen, Sai Ying Pun
A neon cow soon to be added to M+'s collection.

i

ABOUT THE WRITER: Originally from the US, design critic Chen spent four years in Beijing heading up the city's Design Week. He then moved to Hong Kong to serve as the founding curator for architecture and design at the M+ Museum of Visual Culture.

ESSAY 06

Local recall

Mapping an enduring appeal

A former resident relives her time in the city. It includes vivid, visceral memories of vertical living, bustling food markets and trips to the New Territories.

by Liv Lewitschnik, writer

I yearn for Hong Kong more intensely than for any other city in which I've lived. To varying degrees I miss every place I know well and am not currently in. Stockholm because it's where I grew up and where my family is; I miss its green summers and life lived close to the sea. I miss London because of the way its vastness makes me feel overwhelmed and calm all at once. Southern Spain for enveloping me in a rich culture. Queensland for its tropical wilderness and the way it opened my teenage eyes to a world outside the one I was used to. But although I lived in Hong Kong for just three years, it left an impression distinct from any other.

Hong Kong is romantic, unsettling and dramatic. That could be said of many places but Hong Kong combines these attributes on an entirely different level. There's the impossibly vertical architecture, the stormy skies before a typhoon hits, the swirling mass of seven million people and the tiny, hazy, ancient-feeling land they live on. Then there's the tension in the air – now extra ripe with uncertainty as to the city's political future in relation to China – that almost competes with the sometimes-terrible pollution.

I had never been to Hong Kong before saying yes to my posting there as MONOCLE bureau chief in 2010. Stepping off the comfortable air-conditioned Airport Express train at Central, the July heat and humidity hit me like a wall. It made me think of a giant, hot and moist cow's tongue giving the city a perpetual lick.

When I looked towards the sky, only a sliver of blue was showing through the gleaming thicket of glass and steel. These buildings figure prominently in the image

Liv's Hong Kong haunts

01 **Sheung Wan**
Walking through this district is like stepping back in time.

02 **Graham Street Market, Central**
An outdoor market with great produce and street life.

03 **Kubrick, Yau Ma Tei**
Cinema café with a huge film and magazine library.

"Hong Kong would be nothing more than a big shopping centre if it weren't for its street-level self"

that Hong Kong projects to the world: a global city where people live in fast-forward mode; a place where enormous wealth is transferred and amassed; a business hub to end all others in the most strategic part of a fast-growing region.

And it's true that much of Hong Kong life happens up high in these dominant skyscrapers. Within them are intricate mazes of malls, restaurants, spas, gyms, hotels, shops, banks, offices and homes – all stacked on top of each other and connected through walkways and elevators. Hong Kongers have had to learn how to live upward because they have so little ground space to share between them.

That said, Hong Kong would be nothing more than a gigantic shopping centre if it weren't for its street-level self. This is where the unmanicured Hong Kong happens. Here, food markets receive shipments of produce and lorry drivers deliver goods from the Pearl River Delta. Here you realise how many of its old traditions Hong Kong has managed to hold on to, even as the city's green wooden shacks serving wonton noodles and sweet milk tea disappear one by one. Hong Kong's old way of life has been changing for years. Ever since the handover of power from British to Chinese rule in 1997, Hong Kong's future with regard to the PRC has been hanging on a precipice. Hong Kongers poured forth onto the streets in 2014 demanding full democracy and saying no to China's meddling in Hong Kong's politics in the strongest way yet.

I was no longer there to witness the protests but reading and hearing about them from afar made me miss Hong Kong more than ever. Though the political message from the protesters could be heard loud and clear across the world, I was thinking back to everyday life there. Drinking coffee with my future husband on the wide windowsill in our 20th-floor flat on Staunton Street – right on the border between Central and the oldest neighbourhood of Hong Kong, Sheung Wan – seeing the early-morning throng of people already moving far below. They were going to work on the 110-year-old tram, which grated its way through traffic, or in taxis that cost next to nothing and took no time to get almost anywhere.

On weekends we'd go hiking on the trails above Tai Hang, an old low-rise neighbourhood on Hong Kong Island where we rented a tiny rooftop apartment for a while. We'd swim off the beaches of Sai Kung East Country Park. When our families came to visit we would take them to the giant Buddha statue in the New Territories and show off the longest escalator in the world, slowly but surely riding uphill past Hong Kong Island's many great bars and restaurants.

The fact is that I fell in love with Hong Kong over time. Thinking back at how I used to curse at the choking pollution – on some days so bad that you would feel like you had a dreadful hangover despite having not drunk a thing the night before – I never thought the impression would be so enduring. But now I know without doubt that Hong Kong is the city I yearn for. — (M)

i

ABOUT THE WRITER: Liv Lewitschnik is a contributing editor for MONOCLE and previously served as our first bureau chief in Hong Kong. After opening the office in 2010 she left the city in 2013 and now lives in the US.

ESSAY 07

Cut to the chase

New excellence in tailoring

The low cost of setting up shop and an influx of highly skilled practitioners have given rise to a thriving tailoring industry in Hong Kong that is finding favour with a younger generation.

by Mark Cho, shopkeeper and entrepreneur

I have been a tailoring obsessive since I was 16, growing up in London. The bug took hold when I found out that school uniform for seniors allowed a dark coloured suit instead of the standard school blazer and trousers. I started to research tailoring, scouring libraries and shops, and picked the brains of my father and his friends. The more I learned the more complex, interesting and rich the subject became to me.

Being Chinese, Hong Kong came up often in my research. And with good reason: for a man looking to develop his style and build a wardrobe, this may be the ultimate place to start. Apart from virtually every brand in the world now being present here, the city is also home to a large and experienced population of tailors. Spend a few moments on the streets of Tsim Sha Tsui and you will likely be showered with offers to buy a tailor-made suit. This Kowloon neighbourhood has long been home to Hong Kong's tailoring community – at one point, Mirador Mansion on Nathan Road housed 500 tailors.

Today in Hong Kong, passable to very good suits are available with a reasonable price tag (compared to London, Milan and Paris, for example). Therefore there is leeway to experiment with cloth and style, and expand your knowledge. I learnt a great deal first hand: two set of suits, one in 8oz cloth for summer, one in 12oz for winter (thermal luxury); 6.5oz suits are essentially business pyjamas and not worth the expense. All of these experiences were thanks to tailors in Hong Kong.

The roots of the tailoring industry here can be traced back to Shanghai at the turn of the 20th century. Tailors were primarily migrant workers from Ningbo, a much poorer city to the south. Enterprising British tailoring firms had set up branches in Shanghai and trained Ningbo migrants. In 1941, The Shanghai Cutting and Tailoring College was founded and soon it cemented Shanghai's position as a hub for highly skilled tailors. The style and techniques practised by these tailors saw them known as the Red Gang.

"Apart from virtually every brand being present, the city is also home to an experienced population of tailors"

After the Chinese Communist Revolution, many of Shanghai's European expatriates (the tailors' main clientele) relocated to British-run Hong Kong; and with them went the tailors. At the time, Hong Kong already had its own Cantonese tailoring industry with a distinctive identity. While Shanghai tailoring (with its foundation in British and Russian methods) made jackets with a full and shaped chest that was particularly suited to a Caucasian build, Cantonese tailoring was more geared towards the Chinese physique and required less work in shaping the chest. The tailors were known as the Guang Dong Gang.

Best bars for sharp suits

01 Café Gray Deluxe, 88 Queensway
Possibly the best scenic view from a toilet in the world.

02 Red Chamber, 12 Pedder Street
Great cigar and whisky selection.

03 Duddell's,1 Duddell Street
Great decor, as you'd expect from Alan Lo.

As Hong Kong grew, these two types of tailoring flourished side by side. Tailoring itself wasn't a difficult business to get into, assuming you had the skills to produce garments. The cost of rent before the 1980s was reasonable and cloth suppliers were willing to deliver raw materials at an affordable price. As such, starting a tailoring house in Hong Kong required only a small amount of capital.

When Italian fashion and fabrics were introduced to Hong Kong in the 1980s, the city's tailoring experienced a major turning point. The lightweight cloth introduced by the likes of Zegna and Loro Piana contrasted with the heavier fabrics from the English mills; it soon became customers' preferred material and local tailors responded to the demand.

However, the Italian superfine cloth was challenging for the younger, inexperienced tailors. Compared to the heavier British fabric, it was less forgiving of mistakes during construction and did not respond in the same way to steaming and pressing. The challenges of using the new material spurred some tailors to experiment with a new method of constructing jackets using a type of interlining canvas glued into them to provide structure. Although the result was inferior, it was considerably quicker and easier to make the pieces.

From the 2000s onwards Hong Kong's tailors have experienced the tremendous effect of the internet on their business. General knowledge about tailoring is freely available and many of Hong Kong's finest have been identified by the online community as efficient providers of good-quality bespoke garments at a reasonable price. This, coupled with the recent resurgence of interest in suiting in the local market, has made Hong Kong's tailors busier than ever.

Some have also made in-roads into the rest of China, developing workrooms and opening new branches in various parts of the country catering to the modern Chinese consumer and for some, coming full circle from their exodus in the 1940s.

In hindsight, I was fortunate to be able to launch The Armoury in 2010 in Hong Kong; it was probably one of the best places to start from. Retail rents can be reasonable if you are willing to make some compromises. We chose a location that was unused for more than a decade. Shops can be built in China at a decent price and assembled in Hong Kong in no time at all. Given the city's established tailoring industry I was worried that I wouldn't be able to compete. Instead, I found a clientele that was experienced in bespoke garments and able to appreciate the nuances of the Italian and Japanese tailors we use.

It also helps that people in Hong Kong – both long-time residents and recent transplants – are ever active and always happy to try something new. Even a Malaysian-Chinese selling Florentine bespoke tailoring. — (M)

i

ABOUT THE WRITER: Mark Cho is co-founder of The Armoury, a group of menswear shops in Hong Kong and New York, and the co-owner of Drake's in London. He spent his formative years in London, graduated from Brown University in the US then worked in property before his career change to clothing and retail.

ESSAY 08

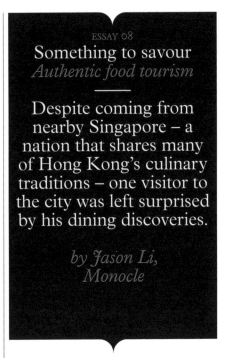

Something to savour

Authentic food tourism

Despite coming from nearby Singapore – a nation that shares many of Hong Kong's culinary traditions – one visitor to the city was left surprised by his dining discoveries.

by Jason Li, Monocle

Ask anyone from Singapore why they're visiting Hong Kong and you'll likely get one or both of two answers: shopping and eating. Well, frankly, I'm not much of a shopper. But I do love a good meal and a country's cuisine is what excites me most when I visit a foreign place.

There's nothing more revealing about a nation's people than their eating habits. Japanese cuisine is marked by a delicate but precise approach, the focus almost always on extracting the natural flavours of the ingredients. Meanwhile, Singapore's equatorial location and ethnic make-up of Chinese, Malays and Indians inform our penchant for wok-fried dishes in spicy and savoury sauces, along with grilled-meat skewers. True, globalisation has made enjoying a bowl of pho just as possible in Toronto as the roadside in Ho Chi Minh City but to truly appreciate a country's cuisine you have to be in the context from which the dish originates.

There's a lot of overlap between Hong Kong and Singapore where food is concerned; we have fine-dining restaurants and street-food options in spades. After putting some thought to the question of what I could get in Hong Kong that I couldn't in Singapore, I arrived at two answers: snake and smelly tofu. If these dishes don't tell me something about Hong Kong, I thought, nothing will.

To be honest, I found snake to be a rather underwhelming affair. I tried it when sat squished between two strangers during lunch hour at Se Wong Yee, a Causeway Bay *cha chaan teng* (tea restaurant). I consumed the rubbery strips of meat without any fuss. It could have been chicken. Afterwards, I followed my nose to a stall on Shanghai Street to sample

Hong Kong dishes

01 **Roast goose**
Succulent meat and crispy skin with plum sauce really sings.
02 **Fish-meat noodles**
The noodles of this soupy dish are made from actual fish meat.
03 **Steamed milk pudding**
Served hot or cold, this sweet custard dessert is said to be good for your skin.

"I found snake to be rather underwhelming – the rubbery strips could have been chicken"

the other item on my list: smelly tofu. The acrid odour comes courtesy of a fermented milk, vegetable and meat marinade. Just before placing my order I hesitated but, in the name of research, I persisted and gingerly took a nibble. Alas, it turns out that smelly tofu is, at the end of the day, still tofu. Don't get me wrong, I enjoyed the contrast of the crusty, savoury skin with the soft flesh of the beancurd but besides the pungency, there was nothing to write home about.

Disheartened by my failed attempt at a culinary adventure in Hong Kong, I had my last meal before my return flight to Singapore in Hing Kee, a non-descript hole-in-the-wall in the Jordan area. I picked something I've eaten a hundred times before back home: a claypot rice with a salted-pork biscuit. After a 15-minute wait, a covered crockpot was brusquely placed in front of me. Whatever was simmering beneath the lid was causing it to tremble. "Wait two minutes," the server ordered.

I felt an unexpected sense of anticipation that only intensified with the unveiling of the contents. The ingredients were strewn casually over a bed of rice, still bubbling as the water evaporated. The earthenware sizzled gleefully when I drizzled soy sauce on it. The caramelised rice at the edge balanced out the saltiness of the meat and because it was cooked over a charcoal stove, a light smokiness permeated everything.

Maybe it was the cooler Hong Kong air but I realised this was no Singapore claypot. Something felt authentic about the experience of digging into dinner hunched over a table by the roadside. Around me were a young couple, a family of four and another lone customer enjoying his pot with a tall bottle of beer. All looked content and blissful. This is how claypot should be eaten, I thought, realising that this is a city that despite having made such advances economically, can still be satisfied by a simple meal.

You see, I'd been approaching this whole food thing all wrong. I found out later from locals that most of them don't eat snake or smelly tofu with any regularity; the foods I thought most unique to Hong Kong did not in fact best represent the city. Instead, the city's personality is found in what's all around: the humble noodle stand, the *tong shui* shop and yes, a simple dish of rice and pork that I witnessed make its way so successfully into the hearts of Hong Kongers. — (M)

i

ABOUT THE WRITER: Singapore-born Jason Li is MONOCLE's deputy bureau chief in Toronto. He is just as happy at a fine-dining establishment as he is at one of Singapore's many open-air food courts.

ESSAY 09

Creating a scene
The meeting of art and food

Far more than just another Hong Kong restaurant and bar launch, The Pawn's revamp – boasting artist collaborations and a modern culinary approach – signals a city on the cusp of a creative resurgence.

by Alan Lo, restaurateur

In 2014 I embarked on what was the most challenging project of my life as a restaurateur: a complete makeover of The Pawn, undoubtedly Hong Kong's most iconic heritage building.

Formerly known as the Woo Cheong Pawn Shop, The Pawn occupies a row of four 19th-century Guangzhou shophouses in the heart of Wan Chai, one of the most famous – or rather infamous – districts on Hong Kong island. My partners at the Press Room Group – Arnold Wong and Paulo Pong – and I have had the privilege of occupying this building since 2008 at the invitation of Urban Renewal Authority to readapt the property for commercial use. It was a dream come true; as a kid I used to imagine what it would be like to have a restaurant inside one of these old buildings.

We proposed a modern British bar and restaurant, appointing Hong Kong-based film director Anothermountainman (Stanley Wong) to create a space that evoked the feeling of a house dating back to the 1950s.

We were also inspired by the spirit and energy of Wan Chai. It is a neighbourhood that's so chaotic yet so real and local. As a restaurant operator, coming to this area was a leap of faith. At the time there were hardly any expats in that part of Wan Chai, let alone quality European food or drink offerings. When we opened in 2008, the project was an instant success. Being the first major restoration development in urban Hong Kong, it was something that received a lot of international attention.

Since then, Hong Kong has become a major arts and creative hub with an important place on the global cultural map. With M+, Hong Kong's new museum of visual culture, on the horizon, as well as Art Basel and a burgeoning art-collecting scene, our city is entering a new cycle.

In the past, when one talked about expats in Hong Kong it often meant bankers and lawyers. Today, Hong Kong attracts the likes of fashion stylists, curators, art dealers, photographers and product designers who are reinvigorating neighbourhoods such as Wan Chai, Tai Hang, Wong Chuk Hang and, more recently, Sham Shui Po.

"Local artists may finally be getting institutional recognition but we felt it was still difficult to see Hong Kong art"

I felt that the makeover of The Pawn needed to reflect this new cycle and provide a platform for the local creative scene. After a two-month renovation we unveiled The Pawn with the same guiding principles. Yet it also had a renewed energy and a new culinary direction led by British chef Tom Aikens, focusing on food provenance, sustainability and organic farming.

We were thrilled to collaborate with Anothermountainman again to curate our art programme. Local artists may finally be getting institutional recognition but we felt it was still difficult to see Hong Kong art unless one had access to private collections. Hence we created a survey of works by some of Hong Kong's best artists for The Pawn's art programme.

Best restaurant artwork

01 The Pawn, Wan Chai "Untitled 2012" by Hong Kong-born, New York-based artist Paul Chan.
02 Duddell's, Central "Time Memory 18" by Japanese artist Shinro Ohtake.
03 Bibo, Sheung Wan Pieces by Jean-Michel Basquiat.

Among the works on show are Chow Chun Fai's signature painted stills from classic Cantonese movies, Firenze Lai's portraits and Angela Su's scientific illustrations. There is also art and architecture collective Map Office's photographic work depicting Hong Kong's shipping containers.

The most controversial work has to be the site-specific video installation by Anothermountainman. He created a set of nine security monitors combining live feeds from various locations in The Pawn and pre-recorded scenes of the artist himself dozing off, a couple having a fight and another making out. While our façade harks back to the past, the interior expresses a narrative reflecting the "nowness" of Hong Kong and the world.

As a restaurateur and art collector, this project is far more than just a restaurant and bar. The revival of The Pawn signals an interesting next 10 years of Hong Kong's creative and cultural development. I can't predict the future but my guess is that it's only going to get more exciting. — (M)

i

ABOUT THE WRITER: Alan Lo is a restaurateur, property developer and leading voice in Hong Kong's art and design scene. With key roles in a number of organisations, including Hong Kong Ambassadors of Design and the global patrons council of Art Basel, he has been a driving force in promoting the city as a cultural hub.

ESSAY 10

Up, down and sideways
Embracing the labyrinth

Getting over the altitude of Hong Kong is one thing; navigating its network of walkways and escalators is quite another. Here's our guide to knowing the city like the back of your hand.

by David Michon, writer

Visit Hong Kong and you're likely to spend a substantial amount of time weaving through crowds as you make your way from dumpling spot to shop, or one meeting to the next. It's not a particularly unusual phenomenon in a big city. But what sets Hong Kong apart is that your feet may never touch the ground.

This city, with one of the world's most impressive collections of skyscrapers, has a unique approach to organising movement. Hong Kong leads the tall-buildings pack in all but the over-300-metres category (an accolade that goes to Dubai) and is home to more than 500 skyscrapers. When you're in urban areas of Hong Kong you find yourself looking way up; at times relentlessly so, as captured by the photographer Michael Wolf in his series *Architecture of Density*: disconcerting large-scale photos of the city's towers.

Hong Kong's tall buildings aren't all silos and in central areas of the city they are enmeshed and indistinguishable for their first several storeys before making a name for themselves on the skyline. From front door to office, your commute is likely to involve navigating tunnels, skywalks, shopping-mall corridors, escalators and lifts that take you from indoor spaces to outdoor ones, public to private, ground level to storeys high. This is compounded by a city that also crashes into hillsides; where third floors connect to first and you're never too sure where you stand unless you're at the top. Hong Kong is, as one recent book argues, a city without ground.

The city took shape piece by piece – not as part of any grand plan – and so these elevated routes have a logic that is rather organic. Yet there is an astonishing efficiency with which people speed their way through this maze. This near-unmappable circuit soon becomes second nature to the Hong Konger and mastering it is essential to finding what's best in this city. Take the tastiest restaurants, for instance. Not often found at street level nor even along the beaten path of upper-level walkways, they're often tucked up on the seventh floor with minimal signage to help you find your way. You may even find yourself thinking, "Wait, this can't be the way..." one or more times before that very last escalator takes you into the heart of dim-sum mania. (Strangely, being high up far from guarantees a view – or windows.)

> *"Your commute is likely to involve navigating tunnels, skywalks, shopping-mall corridors, escalators and lifts"*

What will help you is a familiarity with the complex (read: missing) logic behind this blend of ups, downs, twists and turns. Strangely, it's within this infrastructure that you'll find much of the city's most-used public space. Open areas in malls are your primary meeting points and wider

Best places to escape the escalators

01 Tai O fishing village
Known for its stilt houses that rest above the tidal flats.

02 Tsz Shan monastery
A freshly minted oasis of meditation and reflection.

03 The Nan Lian garden
Verdant and beautiful with Tang dynasty accents.

walkways leading to the next tower are, for some, a perfect place to picnic. Amid the punishing humidity you may be very glad to ditch the roadside and take yourself up a level to enjoy the frigid existence provided by Hong Kong's air-con addiction.

While the polished main shopping areas of the many malls might not give you a sense of the "real" Hong Kong you were hoping to find, in the pathways between them there's a lot to see and do: pop-up lunchtime food stalls, hawkers, salons and exhibitions. On my last pass through the city I caught a karaoke session (at midday) with lots of eager participants.

This city shows us what we were all expecting the future to be: super-dense, sky-high, both gritty and glamorous, a bit intimidating. Despite the humidity or even the rain, there is life at street-level proper. Balancing out the endless escalators and walkways are the streets and alleyways; from the neon-strewn Mong Kok to the quiet and tree-shaded Pound Lane. Hong Kong, despite itself, does street level quite well.

At any level, though, there is one piece of navigating advice to remember: unless you've got time to spare, pay very close attention or you'll never find your way back to the hotel. — (M)

i

ABOUT THE WRITER: Previously producer of *The Urbanist* on Monocle 24, David Michon first visited Hong Kong as interim bureau chief in 2013. He is now editor of architecture and design magazine *Icon*.

ESSAY II

Ebb and flow

The city of contrasts

For all of Hong Kong's cut, thrust and frenetic movement, you can also find moments of serenity and calm that serve as a counterbalance for locals and visitors alike.

by André Fu, architect

I have always considered my home to be a city of juxtaposition. Be it the contrast between old and new or East and West, all aspects of its urban landscape instill a dynamic unlike any other destination in the world. Its uniqueness and endless energy have continued to inspire my creative process.

For those visiting, the immediate impression of Hong Kong's urban credentials is inevitably created by the brilliant airport and its express train service that provides transport to the city centre in a mere 20 minutes. This may be a slice of infrastructure that lacks poetry but it serves as an introduction to the city's uncompromising sense of efficiency and way of life.

For a visitor to Hong Kong – where daily life revolves around its central hub – the modern skyscrapers that are set against lines of high-end retail establishments may appear to lack character. Yet what makes the city unique are the whimsical back alleys where food markets, old pawn shops or tearooms can be discovered. This mismatched quality lends the city its surprising personality.

In the central area, key architectural gems that instantly stand out include IM Pei's Bank of China, the Central Police Station that was revitalised by Herzog & De Meuron as well as the colonial Pedder Building, which is now home to numerous key private-art institutions such as Ben Brown Fine Arts and the Gagosian Gallery.

My all-time favourite piece of architecture is the Hong Kong Club Building by Austrian-born Australian architect Harry Seidler. Completed in 1984, the stone-clad building possesses a unique sculptural quality with a calmly undulating façade.

One of the more recent additions to the urban set is the monolithic 50 Connaught Road. Now home to the Agricultural Bank of China, it's a 28-storey office building by US-based architect Robert AM Stern. Another highlight is the Asia Society Hong Kong Centre at the Old Victoria Barracks: it houses a group of four former British military buildings that were originally built by the British army in the mid-19th century. Today it has been transformed into a cultural institution that offers seasonal exhibitions.

Best-designed spaces

01 **Kadoorie Estate, Kowloon**
An oasis of prewar housing.
02 **The Upper House, Admiralty**
The calm antithesis of the urban hotel experience.
03 **Tai Tam Reservoir**
Unique reservoir set amid lush surrounds.

Besides the major establishments there is also an omnipresent sense of regeneration in a more localised and neighbourhood-driven spirit. I am intrigued by the charming quality of Bridges Street and its adjoining Tai Ping Star Street with its abundance of fun places to eat, delightful florist shops and young art galleries. Within the area is restaurant Yardbird, housed in a charmingly restored postwar Bauhaus-style building, as well as the artful Bibo and Mrs Pound; all examples of Hong Kong's latest generation of small and independent dining offerings.

Despite the fact that life in Hong Kong runs at quite a rapid pace there's the contrasting vast countryside and beaches; ideal for a secluded moment of escape.

The hike around Tai Tam Reservoir is one of my favourite weekend outings. The towering granite dam constructed between 1883 and 1888 is set against breathtaking mountain slopes and lush tree plantations.

Another delightful urban oasis is the Kadoorie Estate along Kadoorie Avenue and Braga Circuit in Kowloon: an exclusive residential community made up of 86 houses and a low-rise apartment block, St George's Court. The Estate spans 80,000 sq m and comprises a tranquil green oasis close to the major business hubs of West Kowloon and Central. This collective of prewar to postmodern houses is a real gem and possibly the most significant representation of the way the city's architecture has evolved through the years. An additional key feature of the Kadoorie Estate is the extensive greenery of mature trees (a true rarity in Hong Kong) that somehow perpetuate a feeling of nostalgia.

"Hong Kong runs at quite a rapid pace. There's the contrasting vast countryside and beaches; ideal for a secluded moment"

Last but not least, the ultimate city escape would have to be The Lawn. It is a secluded garden lounge within the Upper House Hotel that I designed in 2009 and which has become a favourite venue among the art crowd. Many see the purist and tactile quality of the hotel as an honest testament to the new Asian aesthetics; much akin to embracing an antithesis of the city's dramatic pace of life.

This uncompromising sense of juxtaposition has made Hong Kong a city that caters to all tastes and senses. From cutting-edge urban architecture and spots of conserved colonial buildings to its scenic coastal landscapes, it is an unchoreographed collage of intriguing surprises with never a dull moment. — (M)

i

ABOUT THE WRITER: Architect André Fu started his firm Afso to define a modern Asian sensibility. His studio has created a series of globally recognised projects for the likes of Four Seasons Hotels & Resorts, Shangri-La Hotels and Louis Vuitton.

ESSAY 12

New shoots
Compost in the city

Amid the protests that brought Hong Kong to a standstill some friendships blossomed. Knowledge shared between farmers, protestors and onlookers has brought about a new wave of city greening.

by Michael Leung
designer and urban farmer

Top green places

01 Mapopo Community Farm, Fanling
Holds workshops and sells organic food.

02 Occupy Site, Admiralty
A plot of land cared for by the occupiers.

03 Sai Wan Beach, Sai Kung
A beautiful beach with very clean water.

Over the past few years we have seen a huge increase in conventional and urban farming in Hong Kong. Small pockets of concrete have been revitalised to become organic plots and escapes from the pace and stress of the city.

During the first days of the Umbrella Movement in September 2014, urban farming became politicised. After 92 sq m of shrubs were trampled outside the Central Government Complex building in Admiralty, a vacant plot of soil was left at the heart of the protest site where tents and other self-organised communities occupied some of Hong Kong's most important thoroughfares. In Kowloon, at the Mong Kok protest site, 223 small ornamental trees that lined the middle of the normally congested Nathan Road were removed, leaving another vacant plot of soil.

Shortly after the start of the Umbrella Movement some urban farmers decided to intervene with these two plots. Farming became a democratic platform to directly communicate issues such as land and urban redevelopment as well as government and developer collusion.

The roadside planters on Nathan Road were revitalised with seasonal produce. Every day a group of farmers watered the plants, forming new relationships in the process and discussing different environmental and political issues. After the police cleared this Mong Kok site the plants were replaced with the same ornamental trees as before.

A farm was started on the land outside government headquarters. It included tomatoes, potatoes, aloe vera and mint and became a venue for talks and workshops. A food-waste collection system was used to fertilise the soil and the farm attracted many species of wildlife. The day before the site's clearance, farmers decided to donate all their plants to those who visited. By the evening the whole farm was empty.

In the months following the clearance, dozens of tents reoccupied the pavements surrounding the Central Government Complex building in Admiralty. Located between the Democracy Library and a group of protesters' tents, an expanding garden remains to continue the discussion that started during the Umbrella Movement. Seeds and seedlings are being shared alongside communication of urban and rural farming issues in Hong Kong. — (M)

i

ABOUT THE WRITER: Michael Leung is a designer, beekeeper and urban farmer. He focuses on socio-cultural and environmental projects in Hong Kong. His work includes urban agriculture projects such as HK Farm and HK Salt.

Culture
— A guide to the arts

It is a time of significant (and visible) change for Hong Kong's cultural scene. The past few years have seen the opening of outposts from several international galleries as well as thousands of people flocking to the city during spring to attend the Art Basel Hong Kong fair.

On the banks of Victoria Harbour, the government is spending billions on developing the West Kowloon Cultural District. In former industrial areas such as Wong Chuk Hang, residents are working together to create studio and exhibition space to support the work of Hong Kong's young artists.

Over the next few pages we will show you where to find the best of the city's traditional and contemporary culture.

Cinemas
On the big screen

①
Broadway Cinematheque, Yau Ma Tei
Blazing a trail

Hong Kong's film scene may be less buoyant than during the 1980s and 1990s but you wouldn't think so within the walls of Broadway Cinematheque, the city's leading cinema dedicated to independent and arthouse film. Tucked away in Yau Ma Tei's unassuming Prosperous Garden housing estate, it opened in 1996 and houses four 115-seat theatres and a film library, as well as the buzzing Kubrick bookshop and café.

Run by a passionate team of film-lovers who schedule events and screenings around the city, Broadway Cinematheque shows more than 400 titles from 50 countries and hosts nearly 20 film festivals every year, including Hong Kong's Lesbian & Gay Film Festival and the Fresh Wave International Short Film Festival.
Prosperous Garden, 3 Public Square Street
+852 2388 0002
bc.cinema.com.hk

②
Hong Kong Film Archive, Sai Wan Ho
Conserving the classics

Established in 1993, the Hong Kong Film Archive conserves much of the city's cinematic output from a five-storey building on Lei King Road. One part is dedicated to storage (with state-of-the-art systems to preserve old footage); the other includes a cinema and exhibition galleries. Besides sampling local film classics, visitors can also participate in seminars or trace the evolution of the city's cinema in one of the exhibition tours.
50 Lei King Road
+852 2739 2139
filmarchive.gov.hk

③
Agnès B Cinema, Wan Chai
Independence renovated

Part of the Hong Kong Arts Centre, the 119-seat Agnès B Cinema reopened in 2013 after renovations courtesy of the Hong Kong Film Development Fund. Named after the French designer and cinema enthusiast, the theatre champions arthouse and independent films.
2 Harbour Road
+852 2582 0200
hkac.org.hk

④
AMC Pacific Place, Admiralty
Kick back in comfort

The wide leather seats at the AMC, arranged in stadium seating, are among the most comfortable in town and offer plenty of legroom. This and the cinema's well-stocked bar, selling international wines, beers and grown-up snacks, make it one of the smartest places to catch up on recent releases.
L1, Pacific Place Mall
+852 2265 8933
amccinemas.com.hk

Hong Kong on film

01 The Man with the Golden Gun, 1974: While not filmed in its entirety in Hong Kong, this classic Bond offers incredible scenes of the chic city and some surrounding islands during the 1970s. Look out for the famous Peninsula hotel forecourt, a wider Victoria Harbour and the sleazy nightlife of Tsim Sha Tsui.

02 In the Mood for Love, 2000: Few filmmakers are able to set a mood like Wong Kar Wai, a man who has spent years crafting film in the city. This brooding love story between the eternally graceful Maggie Cheung and Tony Leung paints a picture of 1960s Hong Kong that will change your opinion of quite how romantic takeaway noodles can be.

03 Infernal Affairs, 2002: Start watching this and you may get a strange case of déjà vu as the classic Hong Kong thriller was remade by Martin Scorsese in 2006 as *The Departed*. The original is definitely still worth a watch, though. Dark and well crafted, this depiction of a battle between two undercover characters rejuvenated interest in Hong Kong's then-flagging film industry.

04 Election and Election 2, 2005 and 2006: Johnnie To's films on the power struggles within Hong Kong triads (organised-crime gangs) would keep Don Corleone glued to his seat. Filmed all over the city, you'll see neighbourhoods (and activities, we hope) of which you're unlikely to have firsthand experience.

Publications
Pretty in print

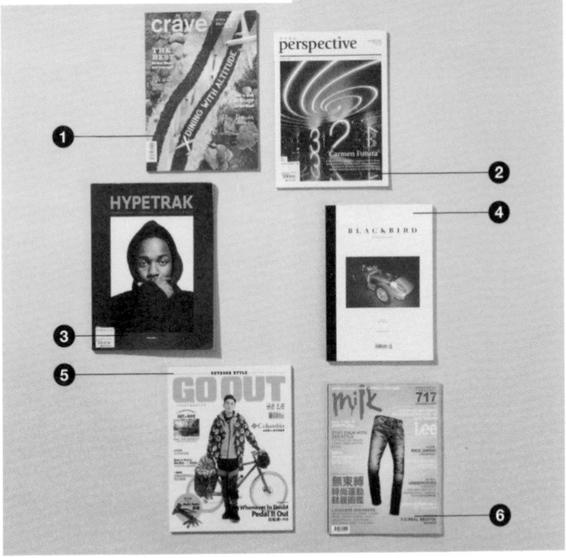

① Media
Reading material

While you're likely to see more Hong Kongers glued to their smartphone screens than a good example of print media, there are a number of impressive publications that prosper in the city. Hong Kong's leading English-language daily is the *South China Morning Post*, which was started in 1903. You can find copies at nearly every convenience shop in the city. For a local take on food and dining pick up a copy of ❶ *Crave*, the city's best monthly dedicated to food reviews, recipes and gastronomic travel stories. For those more interested in Asian architecture and design, ❷ *Perspective* is a bilingual mag that covers global and regional stories. A spin-off of blog, online store and magazine Hypebeast, ❸ *Hypetrak* is dedicated to contemporary global music. Originally operating as a website, the first issue was launched in early 2015.

Tucked behind an unassuming door in Wan Chai is one of the most well-designed and well-stocked private car garages imaginable. It's the home of Blackbird Automotive, which was founded by local resident TK Mak. Its beautiful ❹ *Blackbird Automotive Journal* is a must-read for car fans.

If hiking is your thing, pick up ❺ *Go Out*. Hong Kong's version of this outward bound magazine covers everything from camping to cycling. And finally, if you want to see what the city's cool kids are reading, ❻ *Milk* is a good option for brands and Japanese street style.

② Newsstands, citywide
Get your fix

Kelly and Walsh operates a smart newsstand on the basement level of the Landmark mall and you'll see other newsstands dotted all around the city. Many stock only Chinese-language publications but when in Central look for Cheung Kee (opposite Ralph Lauren) and Tim Kee (outside New World Tower), which both have good international titles.

Private museums
Special collections

1
Liang Yi Museum, Sheung Wan
Antique items

Previously dominated by somewhat dusty government-run institutions and glitzy commercial galleries, Hong Kong has seen the opening of some important private museums over the past couple of years. Leading the charge is the Liang Yi Museum, a family-run collection *(see essay, page 70)* housed across four storeys of a tastefully restored 1960s tenement building on Hollywood Road. Known for its antique shops, the street is a prime location for the museum, which is home to one of the best collections of Ming and Qing-dynasty furniture in the world.

In addition to the Chinese antique furniture on show, Liang Yi also houses an important selection of European clutches, compacts and powder boxes dating from the 1880s to 1960s. The 700-strong collection belongs to Peter Fung, a Hong Kong businessman who has been amassing the items since the 1980s and whose daughter Lynn now directs the museum.
181-199 Hollywood Road
+852 2806 8280
liangyimuseum.com

Home and away

Exhibitions with overseas institutions, such as Paris's Kraemer gallery and London's Victoria and Albert Museum, are run regularly at Liang Yi, as are talks. The interiors are bright and calm and all visitors are guided around the pieces by a specialist.

High ideals

Liang Yi is laid out across four storeys

I wonder if I can swap my camera for that one

2
F11 Photo Museum, Happy Valley
Snap happy

This 80-year-old three-storey art deco building was restored by Douglas So, a former corporate lawyer who, in 2014, opened it as a museum dedicated to both photography and conservation.

Exhibitions are held across the first two floors (Elliott Erwitt was the first photographer to be shown in the museum) while the upper floor houses limited-edition prints, rare photography books and So's vast collection of antique Leica cameras. They range from the 1925 Model A Anastigmat to the latest Leica 100 commemorative cameras.
11 Yuk Sau Street, Happy Valley
f11.com

Public/non-profit art spaces
For all to see

①
Asia Society, Admiralty
From arms to art

Tucked behind Admiralty, near the British Consulate and Island Shangri-La hotel, the Asia Society is a sanctuary within the city. On a site where the British army once housed ammunition, this outpost of the New York-based educational institution is a rare example of architectural preservation in Hong Kong.

Designed by Tod Williams Billie Tsien Architects, the centre opened in 2012 and incorporates four historic military buildings as part of a multi-tier compound that folds into the foothills of Hong Kong Island's steep peak. Exhibitions from Caravaggio to contemporary Southeast Asian artists have been shown and regular performances and screenings are mounted. Even if you're not sure what's on, head up to take in the views from the peaceful rooftop garden. Or grab a meal at restaurant Ammo.
9 Justice Drive
+852 2103 9511
asiasociety.org/hongkong

Load up
Tony Cheng is behind on-site restaurant Ammo

②

Spring Workshop, Wong Chuk Hang
Industrial edge

Wong Chuk Hang, a former industrial district on Hong Kong Island's south side, is fast becoming a must-visit area with great restaurants, retailers and galleries setting up shop in former warehouses and factories. Among the first to put it on the cultural map was Spring Workshop, a non-profit art space founded by Mimi Brown (*pictured*).

Encouraging collaboration between local and international artists and addressing the issue of limited artist space in the city, Spring has three artist-in-residence studios plus an exhibition and performance space, kitchens and outdoor terraces. Spring's large and picturesque terrace is not only a great place to soak up the unique feel of Wong Chuk Hang but also a spot where many of the workshop's artistic projects get started.
3F, Remex Centre,
42 Wong Chuk Hang Road
+852 2110 4370
springworkshop.org

③

Osage, Kwun Tong
Cross-cultural collections

Established in 2004, Osage has become a major platform for exhibiting and promoting Asian contemporary arts over the past decade. Works by artists from Hong Kong, China, Singapore, the Philippines and Thailand are regularly shown in addition to international artists of Asian descent. Through exhibitions and research, founder and director Agnes Lin looks to explore cross-cultural relationships between different countries in Asia as well as the region's global identity.

Set in the up-and-coming district of Kowloon East, Osage is among the largest gallery spaces to be found in the city. The raw warehouse unit shows work across multiple disciplines including performance, installations and interactive multimedia.
4F, Union Hing Yip Factory Building,
20 Hing Yip Street
+852 2793 4817
osagegallery.com

④

Asia Art Archive, Sheung Wan
Resource material

To gen up on contemporary art in the region head to this meticulously organised collection of books and primary reference material housed in an unassuming building in Sheung Wan. Founded in 2000, the AAA manages not only a physical collection but also an online reserve of primary source material from across Asia. To engage the public with contemporary Asian art and its global standing, the archive also hosts workshops, screenings and residencies.
11F, Hollywood Centre,
233 Hollywood Road
+852 2844 1112
aaa.org.hk

⑤

Para Site, Quarry Bay
Critical acclaim

One of Asia's oldest independent art institutions, Para Site opened its new space in Quarry Bay in 2015. It produces regular exhibitions, publications and forums that often encourage critical debate on art and society in and out of Hong Kong.
22F, Wing Wah Industrial Building,
677 King's Road
+852 2517 4620
para-site.org.hk

⑥

Oi!, North Point
Joint ventures

Found in a cluster of heritage-listed buildings built during the early 20th century, the Oi! art space's aim is to provide a calm, creative oasis in the dense North Point neighbourhood. The government-run gallery and studio encourages collaboration between artists and the community through experimental programmes that engage youngsters.
12 Oil Street
+852 2512 3000

Commercial galleries
Art in the city

1

White Cube, Central
Made in Britain

The first White Cube space to open outside of the UK, this expansive two-floor gallery opened in 2012. Offering 550 sq m of exhibition space, the gallery has hosted shows from Gilbert & George, Anselm Kiefer and Antony Gormley. Director Laura Zhou worked previously as the director of Shanghai's ShanghArt Gallery.
50 Connaught Road
+852 2592 2000
whitecube.com

2

Edouard Malingue, Central
Worldwide reach

Having previously operated out of a striking OMA-designed space on Queen's Road Central, in 2015 the Edouard Malingue gallery moved to new digs that occupy an entire floor on Des Voeux Road. Run by Malingue and his wife Lorraine, the gallery is one of the best places to see work from emerging artists from around the world. In addition to mounting solo shows such as Hong Kong's João Vasco Paiva and Cuba's Los Carpinteros, Malingue shows dynamic and international group exhibitions and works on public installations.
6F, 33 Des Voeux Road
+852 2810 0317
edouardmalingue.com

Government-run art venues

01 **Hong Kong Museum of Art, Tsim Sha Tsui:** Houses a large collection of Chinese antiquities and contemporary art and is part of the large cultural development built during the 1990s on the Tsim Sha Tsui waterfront.
hk.art.museum

02 **Hong Kong Museum of History, Tsim Sha Tsui:** Shows engaging exhibits and dioramas to give visitors an understanding of Hong Kong's past.
hk.history.museum

03 **Flagstaff House Museum of Tea Ware, Central:** Houses a rare Chinese teaware collection and educates visitors on its history, all within Hong Kong Park.
hk.art.museum

3

Galerie du Monde, Central
Pledge to paintings

One of Hong Kong's oldest contemporary-art galleries, Galerie du Monde opened in 1974 and today is known for a commitment to ink paintings on paper. An eye-opener on the scope and skill of contemporary Chinese work.
108 Ruttonjee Centre,
11 Duddell Street
+852 2525 0529
galeriedumonde.com

4

Pedder Building galleries, Central
All in one

Trust Hong Kong to have found a way to create what could be considered a luxury shopping centre for contemporary art. If you're in the mood for culture but pressed for time, head to the Pedder Building: a historic nine-storey edifice in the heart of Central that is home to some of the city's best commercial-art galleries.
12 Pedder Street

Culture core
The Pedder Building is a stunning art hub

Pedder Building highlights

01 Gagosian: Opened in 2010, this is the only Asian location of the contemporary-art powerhouse run by Larry Gagosian. Launching the space with a show by Damien Hirst, the large gallery on the Pedder Building's seventh floor has mounted shows with work from Richard Prince, Cy Twombly and Jean-Michel Basquiat, making it a great place to start your tour.

02 Lehmann Maupin: Another transplant from the US, Lehmann Maupin's OMA-designed Hong Kong outpost on the fourth floor is a must-see space. Divided into two exhibition areas, the ubiquitous white gallery walls contrast with rough, exposed beams and a central column that draw attention to the Pedder Building's long history. David Maupin and Rachel Lehmann have given several of their artists their first Hong Kong exhibitions in the space, including Asian luminaries such as Do Ho Suh and Lee Bul.

03 Pearl Lam: Housed on the sixth floor, Pearl Lam's first Hong Kong space (a second one opened in Sheung Wan in 2015) is dedicated to exhibiting both Asian and western art. Solo exhibitions have ranged from Chinese artists such as Su Xiaobai and Zhu Jinshi to the UK's Yinka Shonibare and Jim Lambie.

04 Hanart TZ: Johnson Chang has been leading the contemporary-art charge in Hong Kong since 1983. That's when he opened his first Hanart space to display art from China and its diaspora that was unfamiliar to Hong Kong eyes. Having held politically important exhibitions during the late 1980s, Chang's fourth-floor space remains a place where contemporary Chinese art is displayed and discussed.

05 Simon Lee: In 2012, Mayfair-based Simon Lee Gallery opened its Hong Kong space under the directorship of Katherine Schaefer. Since opening, Schaefer and her team have worked in the space with new artists that include the likes of André Komatsu and Daido Moriyama.

06 Ben Brown Fine Arts: Designed by André Fu, Ben Brown's space was the first London gallery to open in the Pedder Building. It has since hosted exhibitions from artists such as Ron Arad, Candida Höfer, Caio Fonseca and Hong Kong's Simon Birch.

West Kowloon Cultural District

You can't talk to anyone about the state of culture in Hong Kong and not hear about the development of the West Kowloon Cultural District. By 2020 the development – one of the world's largest of its type – will bring a contemporary-art museum, performing-arts venues and green space to a large parcel of land that juts out into Victoria Harbour from below the ICC Tower. The first building to open will be the Xiqu Centre in 2017: the world's largest venue dedicated to the preservation, development and performance of traditional Chinese theatre. Three years later, it will be joined by a second performance space: the Lyric Theatre.

In 2018 the much-anticipated M+ museum for visual culture will open. Led by Lars Nittve (the former director of Stockholm's Moderna Museet and the founding director of London's Tate Modern), the curators of M+ are already building the permanent collection. It will include items from Shiro Kuramata's 1988 "Kiyotomo Sushi Bar" to the Uli Sigg collection – arguably one of the best representations of contemporary Chinese art – and Asia's first dedicated architectural collection.

The M+ building has been designed by Herzog & de Meuron. While changeable due to construction, the West Kowloon waterfront promenade is open to the public daily and is the site of regular events and festivals. Pop over to the new district while it's still in progress for a glimpse of Hong Kong's cultural future.

Nearest MTR stations: Kowloon, exit D and Austin, exit D2

Cultural festivals
Tales of tradition

Roaring success — The Fire Dragon Dance is not to be missed

① Mid-Autumn Festival, citywide
Mooncakes and dragons

One of the biggest events on the Chinese calendar, this is the time of year for mooncakes: a pastry filled with an egg yolk and lotus-seed custard. The best are made at the Peninsula's Spring Moon.

In Tai Hang village (*see page 136*) residents continue to perform their famous Fire Dragon Dance that was started in the 19th century and has earned a place in China's cultural heritage.

The parade winds its way through the small streets, filling them with the sound of beating drums and the smell of smoke. It's likely to be packed but it is well worth tolerating the crowd.

Usually in September

② Tuen Ng Festival, citywide
Set sail

This holiday commemorates the story of a man who drowned himself to protest corrupt leaders 2,000 years ago. At Hong Kong's many beaches, locals go for a swim in his honour. *Zongzi* (glutinous rice dumplings) are the traditional food but the biggest draw for visitors are the Dragon Boat Races that have been taking place here since the mid-1970s.

Attracting many thousands of competitors from around the world, ornate canoe-like boats are powered by paddlers who race to the sound of loud drums. The unofficial races at Stanley are a spectacle; a noisy, seafaring regatta.

Usually in June

Maybe I bought too many balloons...

③

Chinese New Year, citywide
Fresh start

Arguably the biggest holiday on the Chinese Lunar calendar. Being in Hong Kong during Chinese New Year may not be the most efficient plan for doing business as many offices are closed. But it is a great time to feel the city's traditional culture at full speed.

Head to Prince Edward flower market in Kowloon, which will be full of colourful and auspicious blooms that Hong Kongers believe bring good fortune. Step into one of the shops selling traditional *lai see*: mostly red envelopes that are filled with bank notes and exchanged between acquaintances; you may find yourself at the receiving end of one or two. And if you're in town for meetings, be sure to fill up a few envelopes with fresh bank notes (but no sums that feature the unlucky number four) to hand out to junior colleagues.

Cantonese restaurants will be jammed but head in to try foods such as *nin gao* (a steamed sticky cake) or *ho si* (dried oysters); foods with names that translate into fortuitous meanings. There is also a fireworks display over Victoria, best viewed from a boat or bar with great views such as Café Gray Deluxe.
Between late January and mid February

④

Harbour illuminations
Night lights

Even if there's not a festival on when you visit you can catch a view of the daily light show that illuminates the harbour every evening at 20.00. Stay away from the crowded tourist vantage points on Tsim Sha Tsui and Wan Chai harbour fronts and leave the masses behind when you book yourself a boat for an evening cruise of the harbour.

Radio and podcasts
On the waves

RTHK
Broadcast central

Founded in 1923, RTHK is the city's oldest broadcaster and the only one that operates as a public service. Working across television, online and radio, it's the latter you'll most likely come across, either in its Cantonese form (perhaps in a taxi cab) or on RTHK3, the city's leading, live English-language radio service.

Available live or via podcast, our top picks include *Phil Whelan's Morning Brew*, which is live every weekday from 09.00 to 13.00 and covers various aspects of daily Hong Kong life and culture. It's the perfect thing to tune in to to find out what the city's really talking about. *Hong Kong Today* is where you get your fill of current affairs and news; you can start your day there from 06.30 on weekdays.

A podcast to hunt down is Anna Healy Fenton's *Peaks and Troughs*, a 12-part series that was originally broadcast in early 2015 and explored life in Hong Kong, looking at everything from where the city's older expats end up to issues of wine fraud and little-known stories about the harbour.

Listen in

Tucked behind the Monocle Shop in Wan Chai, our Hong Kong bureau broadcasts live on Monocle 24. We'll keep you up to date with the latest happenings in the city, from culture and design to politics and business. Tune in at *monocle.com/radio*.

Private clubs
High society

Places to get invited to

01 **The Foreign Correspondents' Club, Central:** With its foundations in a single group of journalists who rallied together in Chongqing in 1943, the FCC (*see essay, page 74*) is a bustling meeting place for many in media, diplomacy and business. In its iconic main bar, slowly whirring ceiling fans and wood-shuttered windows transport guests to another time. Non-journalists face a near three-year waiting list but visiting journalists and correspondents can sign up for a temporary pass.
2 Lower Albert Road

02 **The China Club, Central:** David Tang's high-society bolthole at the top of the Old Bank of China Building feels a bit like a 1930s Shanghai den of decadence. It is billed as a members' club but good hotel concierges should be able to book you a table for dinner.
1 Bank Street

Performing-art spaces
Show-stopping scenes

①
Hong Kong City Hall, Central, and Hong Kong Cultural Centre, Tsim Sha Tsui
Across the harbour

If you've booked yourself a ticket to see one of the city's orchestras or catch a performance by visiting musicians, chances are you'll be heading to Hong Kong City Hall or Cultural Centre: two important institutions almost directly opposite each other across Victoria Harbour. Important parts of the city's cultural landscape, these two venues have played host to some of the world's best-known companies, including the New York Philharmonic Orchestra and Beijing's Peking Opera troupe.

Built in 1962 on part of the reclaimed waterfront abutting Victoria Harbour, Hong Kong's City Hall was the first multi-use cultural complex in the city. Divided into two spaces that surround a memorial garden, it's one of the best examples of Bauhaus-inspired architecture in Hong Kong and is home to a large recital hall as well as a smaller studio and exhibition rooms.

Across the harbour, Hong Kong's Cultural Centre was built more than 20 years later yet remains a controversial building on the harbour. Constructed on a site that required the demolition of a historic railroad station, it includes a large concert hall (home to the Hong Kong Philharmonic and the largest pipe organ in Asia), two theatres and an exhibition and rehearsal space.

If you want to catch a recital, ballet or play while in town, be sure to check out the schedules of these two venues.

Hong Kong City Hall:
5 Edinburgh Place
+852 2921 2840
lcsd.gov.hk/en/hkch/index.html
Hong Kong Cultural Centre:
10 Salisbury Road
+852 2734 2009
lcsd.gov.hk/hkcc

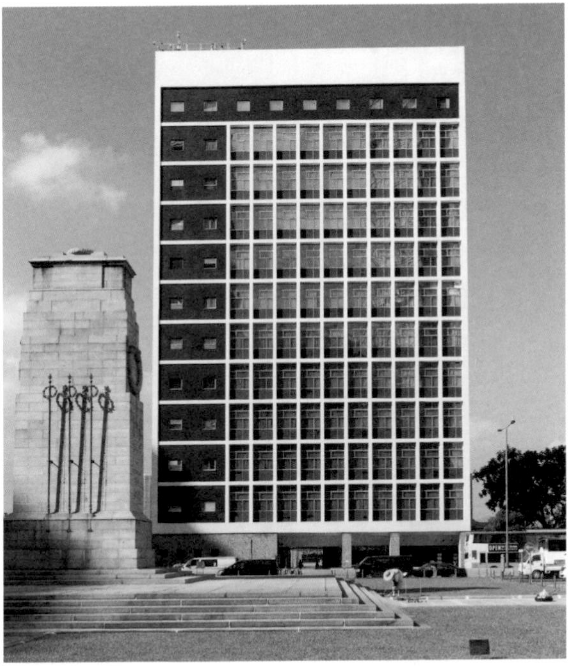

Built to last

The Culture Centre has stood for two decades

②

Chinese opera, various locations
Age-old legends

An unmistakeable part of Hong Kong culture, Chinese opera is an experience unlike any other. Among the oldest dramatic art forms in the world, these operatic performances are a spectacle of colourful costumes and melodic singing that bring Chinese traditional legends to life. Sometimes this includes acrobatics and martial arts, too.

Although Chinese opera is no longer as popular, an effort is made to keep the tradition alive. Despite financial struggles, North Point's legendary Sunbeam Theatre – where performances have taken place for more than 40 years – still stands as the city's last independent theatre for the industry. And in 2012, Hong Kong's only surviving prewar cinema building in Yau Ma Tei was reopened as a venue dedicated to Cantonese opera. For fans of the genre – or simply those curious to see what it is all about – performances are staged regularly at both venues.

Sunbeam Theatre:
423 King's Road, North Point
+852 2563 2959
sunbeamtheatre.com
Yau Ma Tei Theatre:
6 Waterloo Road, Yau Ma Tei
+852 2264 8108
lcsd.gov.hk/en/ymtt

Shining light
—
Sunbeam Theatre is a Hong Kong institution

新光戲院大劇場
預 ADVANCE 售 即 NOW 售 預 ADVANCE 售 即 NOW 售

星海留痕
現代教育
酒家
馬寶道 33
Wellcome 惠康
金胎蝴蝶夢
SUNBEAM THEATRE
新光

Design and architecture

— Sights for sore necks

Behold Hong Kong's skyline in all its skyscraper glory. It's hard to imagine that this spectacular vista took less than half a century to materialise but it's emblematic of the city's relentless march towards modernity. Speak to people who knew Hong Kong a few decades ago and many will tell you that even Victoria Harbour looks smaller – the result of land reclamation on both sides of the waterway.

But this city isn't one that will let go of its past easily. Hong Kong is marked by an eclectic confluence of archaic and futuristic, deliberate and accidental, all of which can make exploring the city a dizzying experience.

Which is where this section comes in. The following pages catalogue our favourite examples of architecture and design, among them buildings, parks and visual icons. We also take stock of smart urban infrastructure that helps citizens get from A to B efficiently. So strap on some walking shoes and join us on a tour of Hong Kong's most compelling sights.

Historic and traditional buildings
An ancient heritage

1
Wong Tai Sin Temple, Chuk Yuen Village
Ceramic-clad shrine

Often sandwiched between modern buildings, Hong Kong's Chinese temples regularly outlast many of their secular counterparts. During festivals and Chinese New Year, locals flock to these traditional places of worship to seek good fortune through offerings and rituals.

Built in 1921, the Wong Tai Sin temple is home to Taoism, Buddhism and Confucianism. Marked by their Oriental curved eaves, Chinese engravings and statues of Chinese deities standing guard, there is a shrine dedicated to every god imaginable. Among them is Lo Pan, the patron deity of builders, architects and carpenters, who has a temple built in his honour in Kennedy Town. Contractors and tradesmen continue to come here to seek his blessing to this day.

2 Chuk Yuen Village, Wong Tai Sin
+852 2327 8141
siksikyuen.org.hk

②
Po Lin Monastery, Lantau Island
Popular sanctuary

Initially built as a small temple by monks visiting from China's Jiangsu province, Po Lin Monastery has since grown to become one of Hong Kong's most important Buddhist sanctums. Perched on Lantau Island's Ngong Ping plateau, the monastery has expanded significantly from its earliest days as a thatched hut to include several shrine halls and courtyards. A brief walk from the Po Lin Monastery is another landmark known as the Wisdom Path: a series of 38 columns engraved with the Heart Sutra prayer that forms a figure of eight.
Ngong Ping
+852 2985 5248
plm.org.hk

Ah. Not the best place to try to make a cup of tea

Enduring traditions

01 **Feng shui:** The Chinese tradition of arranging things to foster prosperity and good luck, feng shui still holds currency in Hong Kong. Some attribute the city's economic success to its auspicious geographical location at the confluence of China's southern mountain ranges, thought to be spiritual dragons. Most of the glassy towers that make up the skyline were designed, oriented and built in consultation with esteemed masters of the craft. For instance, the Jardine House, nicknamed "Thousand Hole Building", sports rows of circular windows meant to usher in wealth. Meanwhile, in Central, visitors can rub the paws of the two bronze lions perched by HSBC's entrance (which almost became scrap metal during the Japanese occupation of Hong Kong in the 1940s) to improve their personal fortune.

02 **Paper shops on Queen's Road West:** The shops selling paper offerings on Queen's Road West stand out for their red lanterns and joss incense spiralling down the shop frames. They are a reflection of how Hong Kong has managed to retain its culture while embracing all that modernity brings. Here you can find paper replicas of just about anything – mobile phones, mansions and even pets – that people purchase and then set aflame. The belief is that the deceased receive these gifts and are then able to live their afterlife in material comfort.

3

Walled City Park, Kowloon
New oasis

Formerly a military station used by the Qing government, Kowloon's Walled City was left in a semi-lawless state when British troops took over Hong Kong in 1898. In the decades that followed it became home to 33,000 residents packed into decaying quarters and was a hotbed for crime and prostitution.

This colourful part of Hong Kong was demolished in 1994 and an urban oasis modelled after the Jiangnan gardens of the early Qing Dynasty has been built in its place. Remnants from the military fort, including old wells and cannons, can still be found inside the park.
Tung Tsing Road
lcsd.gov.hk

Tsz Shan Monastery

More often than not, when one of the city's tycoons constructs a new building the result is a soaring steel office tower that further cements their business prowess via the Hong Kong skyline. But over in Tai Po – an area of the New Territories that's about 30 minutes from Central – one of the city's most influential businessmen has spent years building a remote monastery that he hopes will bring some peace and quiet to the often frantic lives of Hong Kongers.

Across an area of nearly five hectares, Li Ka-Shing (Asia's richest man) has built the Tsz Shan Monastery, a Buddhist community home that features a 76-metre-high bronze statue of Guan Yin, the goddess of mercy, that is set to become one of Hong Kong's new visual marvels.

Run by Li Ka-Shing's foundation, the monastery will only permit 500 visitors per day; spots must be reserved in advance and tour groups are not allowed. The monks and nuns in residence hail from all over the world and the monastery will host regular educational programmes. In a city where many spiritual sites are overrun by tourists, the Tsz Shan monastery aims to provide a peaceful place for Hong Kongers.

tszshan.org

Colonial leftovers
Trappings of power

1
PMQ, Central
Creative revival

Built in 1951, the Hollywood Road Police Married Quarters housed staff and their families for close to five decades. After years of lying empty, a decision was made to transform the site into a creative-industries landmark showcasing Hong Kong craft and design.

Embodying postwar modernist architecture, PMQ's buildings have been refurbished and upgraded (*above*). Residential units have been converted into studios and shops while the atrium has been adapted into an exhibition and event space. PMQ is a rare example of building conservation in the city.

35 Aberdeen Street
pmq.org.hk

2
St George's Building, Central
Ornate statement

Originally designed by Hong Kong-based architecture firm Leigh and Orange in 1904, St George's Building was overhauled in 1969 but still retains its avant-garde bronze and aluminium exterior. The choice of material helps keep the insides of the retail and office block cool during the humid summer months.

The building's pièce de résistance is its striking grand lobby, which is made from Serpeggiante marble and provides the cavernous space with a warm, inviting atmosphere. The lift area, segregated by two decorative Murano glass screens, is also worth a look.

2 Ice House Street

③

Lugard Road, Victoria Peak
Architects' avenue

A study of 20th-century western architecture ranging from Scottish Baronial to art deco and Bauhaus, the houses along Lugard Road are undoubtedly worth a look. The oldest – number 27 – is a stately, neoclassical two-storey manor built in 1914 and designed by British architect Lennox Godfrey Bird.

In 2012, hotel developer Ashley Pacific bought the premises with plans to convert it into a boutique hotel, a move that has raised ire among many. Number 28 next door was also designed by Bird, who lived in it from 1924 until the end of the Second World War.
Lugard Road

④

Old Bank of China Building, Central
Former glory

Before Bank of China moved its headquarters to the glitzy IM Pei-designed skyscraper, this 17-storey granite edifice on Des Voeux Road was its home. Built by UK firm Palmer and Turner soon after the Communist party had come into power in China, the building quickly became a matter of national pride.

Upon completion in 1950 it was the city's tallest tower, peaking above its rival Hong Kong Bank. Take a step back in time by visiting the China Club on the top three floors, which resembles a 1930s Shanghainese teahouse.
1 Bank Street

The most interesting news today is that I'm on my 28th cup of tea

Lasting legacy

01 **English-style postboxes:** Vintage letterboxes can still be found in use across the city but after the handover of Hong Kong to China, these iconic (once-red) postboxes were repainted green and purple to represent the colours of Hong Kong Post. Today only 58 of these colonial-era post boxes – etched with the insignia of the monarch at the time – are still in operation, ranging from pillar letterboxes to wall boxes.

02 **Pottinger Street stalls:** For more than half a century, vendors have been setting up their stalls on the granite steps of Pottinger Street leading down towards Queen's Road, hawking everything from flowers to cheap souvenirs. Locals affectionately call it Stone Slab Street and the makeshift booths have become a permanent fixture. Its atmospheric setting has made this pedestrian-only strip ideal for many films, TV dramas and advertisements. And while Pottinger might be the most famous market, there are plenty of smaller ones worth exploring.

Metropolitan landmarks
Above and beyond

①

Pacific Place Mall, Admiralty
Rooftop oasis

In 2011, British designer Thomas Heatherwick completed his overhaul of Pacific Place, a luxury shopping mall and office building that was built in 1988. Using tactile materials such as stone and bronze, the interior is far more charming than your average shopping centre.

Our favourite spot has to be the beautifully simple rooftop garden where customers can soak up the sun and relax. Glass skylights installed on the garden's floor allow for natural light to flood the interiors below, which helps to maximise the sense of space.
88 Queensway
+852 2844 8988
pacificplace.com.hk

The Hopewell Centre's shape is a rare sight

Um, can I read my newspaper on the ground floor instead?

2

Hopewell Centre, Wan Chai

Ahead of the curve

Although its title of Asia's tallest tower has since been lost to the Bank of China Tower, the 216-metre-tall Hopewell Centre – completed in 1980 – is one of the world's few cylindrical skyscrapers. Today the building's 62nd-floor revolving restaurant still stands out for its sweeping views of the city.

183 Queen's Road East

hopewellcentre.com

In the round

Built on a steep slope, the front, ground-floor entrance to the building is on Queen's Road East while the back opens onto Kennedy Road from the 17th floor. Every storey follows a circular floor plan; there's even a private circular swimming pool on the roof.

3

IM Pei Bank of China, Central

Imposing figure

Masterminded by Pritzker laureate IM Pei this tower, which reaches 370 metres into the clouds, is one of the most distinguishable silhouettes on the skyline thanks to its angular shape, reflective glass exterior and strips of light that dissect the surface every night. While this is the Bank of China's HQ, the 43rd-floor observation deck is open to the public.

One of the rare buildings in Hong Kong to be erected without the consultation of feng shui masters, Pei's design was initially met with criticism but has since become a key part of the cityscape.

1 Garden Road

bochk.com

Bamboo scaffolding
Keeping the city growing
Everything from Hong Kong's tallest skyscrapers to its low-level shop houses owe their existence to humble bamboo and the scores of workers who use it to build scaffolding. Significantly faster to assemble than steel scaffolding and lighter to transport, the speed at which bamboo scaffolders can do their job – up to 100 sq m per hour, per person – helps enable Hong Kong's rapid rate of construction.

The workers operate in groups to build stable structures that reach as high as the project demands; even the gargantuan International Commerce Centre was constructed using bamboo scaffolding. The tools needed besides bamboo and nylon tie-fasts are surprisingly minimal: a hard hat, a safety harness and two knives for cutting the bamboo and rope. While there's much to be admired about Hong Kong's economic development, more credit should be paid to these unsung heroes.

Green spaces
Outdoor attractions

①
Masonry Wall, Sheung Wan
Taking root

Sometimes the most intriguing sights in a city are not intentional. Take the masonry-wall trees along Hollywood Road in Sheung Wan for instance. These vertical concrete walls were erected more than a century ago to prevent mudslides in the hilly terrain but 14 banyan trees have since taken root and refused to let go. Not that anyone is complaining: their expansive crowns provide shade for pedestrians and are one of the few signs of nature left in a concrete jungle. Not to mention the fact that the intricate web woven by the crisscrossing of roots is impressive to behold.

These trees have securely anchored themselves in the walls as well as the hearts of people who live here. The passion for them runs deep: in 2005, residents successfully petitioned for their conservation when the plot of land was sold.
Hollywood Road

②
Street garden, Star Street
Signs of life

Finding a spot of green is hard amid the high-rises but it's not impossible. Dotted across the city are street gardens between blocks of flats or tucked away in unexpected nooks. In fact there's one in the Star Street precinct (*see page 134*) just around the corner from our bureau.

These communal civic spaces – often marked by shady trees in brick planters – are where many seniors spend their mornings doing tai chi. In the afternoon you can see housewives swapping gossip and retirees playing chess. It's a smart use of space that counteracts the isolation that can come about from living in such a dense city.
starstreet.com.hk

③
Public exercise equipment, citywide
Fit for purpose

Brightly coloured outdoor exercise equipment is scattered around parks and walking trails across the city. Ostensibly targeted at helping citizens keep fit, these weather-resistant metal ellipticals and stretching bars are mostly used by elders in the early mornings and evenings when the air is cooler. They're also the perfect warm-up and starting point for a daily run.

Infrastructure
Unique urban forms

1

Tong laus
Low-rise residences

Found in some of the city's oldest neighbourhoods – such as Sham Shui Po, where little has changed for decades – *tong laus* are a reminder of how the city once looked. These two to five-storey buildings are recognisable by their slim street frontages and long narrow rooms. Many were built as shop houses where the owner would sleep above his shop and the floors above that would be rented out. But when the Chinese Civil War hit in the middle of the 20th century these buildings became makeshift homes for fleeing refugees. Under threat from demolition, *tong laus* stand in stark contrast to the city's skyscrapers.

2

Old neon signs
Bright sparks

Amid the frantic pace of life in Hong Kong it's easy to overlook the painted shop signs that line the walls of tenement buildings or their neon counterparts that rest over busy thoroughfares. With old businesses closing down and no one to care for these markers, old shop signs are quickly vanishing across Hong Kong's cityscape.

Although these old-school fixtures are less common today they can still be spotted in older neighbourhoods such as Jordan and Sham Shui Po. In particular, look out for traditional shops where the Chinese calligraphy on plaques and signs was either painted or carved by hand.

3

Apartment towers
Vertical living

The majority of the population live in high-rise apartment blocks; a necessity given Hong Kong's limited land mass. Some find their façades dour and mind-numbingly uniform in appearance; others find them full of character. Either way, these conglomerations of cellular living units with bamboo poles of laundry jutting out from the windows have come to represent the quintessential living experience of the city. Photographers from around the world, such as German Michael Wolf and David Elliott from Canada, have captured the hive-like quality of these blocks that, thankfully, are dressed with a fresh coat of paint every so often.

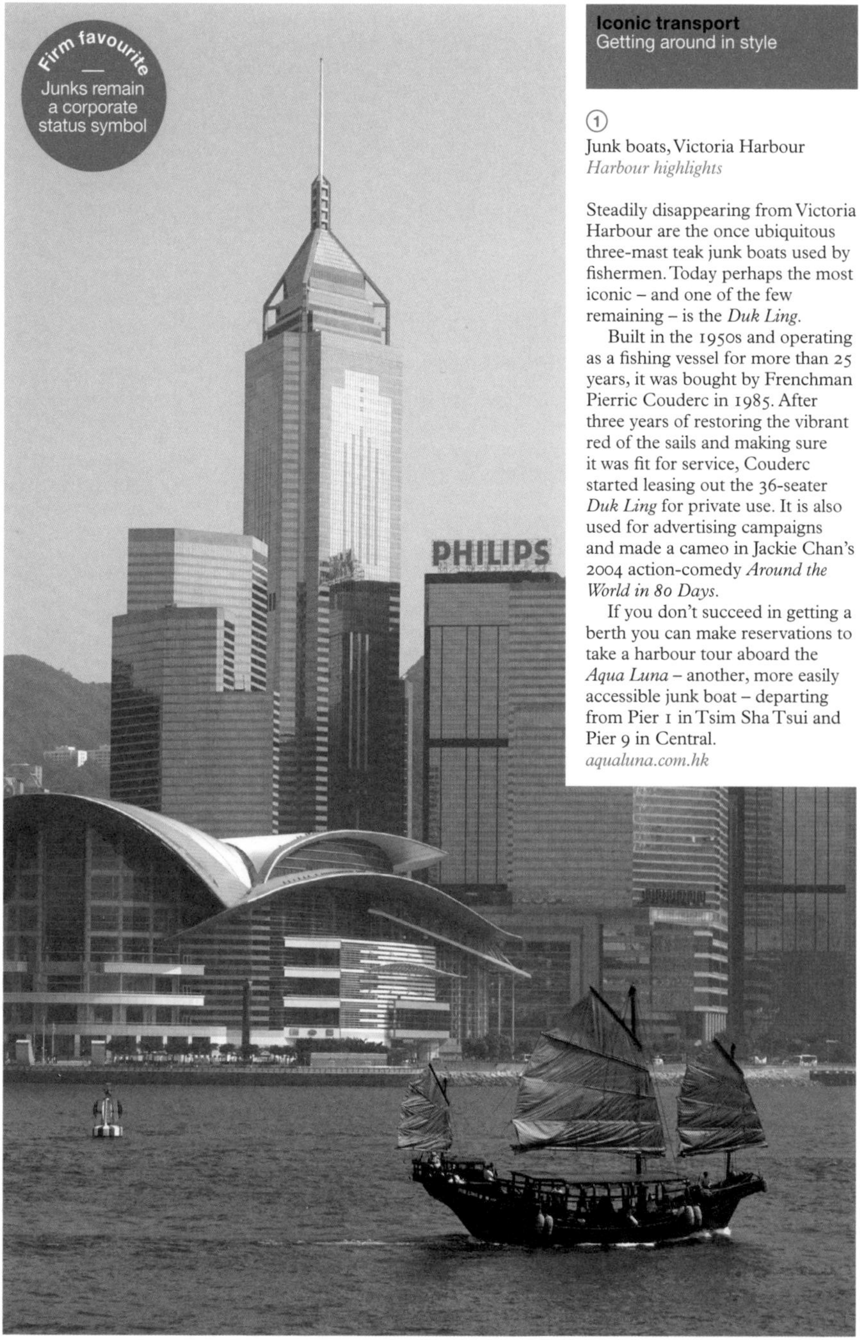
Firm favourite
Junks remain a corporate status symbol
PHILIPS

Iconic transport
Getting around in style

①
Junk boats, Victoria Harbour
Harbour highlights

Steadily disappearing from Victoria Harbour are the once ubiquitous three-mast teak junk boats used by fishermen. Today perhaps the most iconic – and one of the few remaining – is the *Duk Ling.*

Built in the 1950s and operating as a fishing vessel for more than 25 years, it was bought by Frenchman Pierric Couderc in 1985. After three years of restoring the vibrant red of the sails and making sure it was fit for service, Couderc started leasing out the 36-seater *Duk Ling* for private use. It is also used for advertising campaigns and made a cameo in Jackie Chan's 2004 action-comedy *Around the World in 80 Days.*

If you don't succeed in getting a berth you can make reservations to take a harbour tour aboard the *Aqua Luna* – another, more easily accessible junk boat – departing from Pier 1 in Tsim Sha Tsui and Pier 9 in Central.
aqualuna.com.hk

2

Walkways and escalators, Central
One-upmanship

Hong Kong's city slickers know that the most efficient way of getting around Central on foot is not at ground level but one floor up in the intricate network of elevated walkways. It all started in the 1970s when a developer decided to link up a hotel to the second floor of the shopping centre next door. Soon the government expanded the approach and connected residential complexes to shopping centres to transport hubs, including the Central MTR Station and Central ferry piers.

Over the years these skywalks have become unexpected public civic spaces in their own right. There are adjoining gardens that present a quick escape for office workers in search of some peace and quiet; on Sundays the segment near the ferry terminal transforms into a picnic ground for the island's domestic helpers to enjoy on their day off.

Fast thinking

The Mid-Levels escalator that runs from 100 Queen's Road Central to Conduit Road is the longest outdoor escalator system in the world. Stretching over 800 metres, a one-way ride from end to end takes 20 minutes (if you just stand for the whole journey).

Buena vista
Identify the city's skyline from Victoria Peak

3

Peak Tram, Central

Retro rail link

Before ferrying tourists up and down Hong Kong's most famous hill, Victoria Peak, the city's oldest public transport played a crucial role in providing a swift way for the 30 to 40 families living up there during the 19th century to get in and out. Designed in 1888 by Scotsman Alexander Findlay Smith, the first 30-seater carriages were constructed from varnished timber and powered by coal-fired steam boilers.

The version today holds up to 120 passengers and stops at six stations, pausing at select vantage points where the foliage has been cleared to allow passengers to take snapshots of the breathtaking vista. The vehicle retains its signature steep floor angled against the slope it travels upon, creating an optical illusion of buildings tilting towards the peak.

33 Garden Road
+852 2522 0922
thepeak.com.hk

4

City trams

Streetcars desired

For more than a century the city's trams have shuttled residents along the north side of Hong Kong Island from as far as Shau Kei Wan in the east to Kennedy Town in the west. Although by no means the swiftest way to get around the city, they hold an important place in Hong Kong culture.

From early morning until midnight these double-decker wooden-framed streetcars amble their way through the city's busiest streets for a flat rate of HK$2.30. More recently, a modern air-conditioned version of the ding-ding (as it is fondly known here) has also been introduced. Aside from being a charming way to get from one place to another they're a great way to tour Hong Kong's sometimes haphazard streets. Try to grab a top-deck seat for the best views. There are even some older trams that you can rent for the evening and dine in.

hktramways.com

MTR graphics
Sign of the times
Among the most efficient public-transportation networks in the world, the MTR subway system is indispensable for getting around Hong Kong. In operation since 1979, over the years the MTR has developed a coherent signage and graphic identity characterised by simple, distinctive designs.

A team of 20 in-house designers are responsible for all of MTR's branding needs. Throughout the network, all station names and signposts are written in the Myriad typeface, while the MTR has commissioned a special font called MTR Song for station lettering in Chinese. New pictograms have also been added to reflect societal changes, such as the introduction of priority seats on trains.

Word to the wise

Aside from the MTR's iconic visual identity, visitors will find it hard to ignore the system's audio messages that – among other things – remind Hong Kongers to avoid accidents on escalators by looking up from their mobile phones from time to time.

⑤
Ngong Ping cable car, Lantau Island
High ideals

This 25-minute cable-car journey takes passengers from Tung Chung MTR Station through the picturesque hills of Lantau Island to the only other stop on the trip: Ngong Ping. Riders can choose between standard cabins or "crystal cabins", which feature a glass floor for a view of the flora and fauna below. Ngong Ping is where visitors will find the Po Lin Monastery, which houses the famous Tian Tan Buddha. The 34-metre-tall statue has been sitting in lotus position overlooking the island from the top of a long flight of steps since 1993.
Ngong Ping
+852 3666 0606
np360.com.hk

❻
Star Ferry, various locations
Crest of a wave

There are few better ways to spend HK$2.50 than to take a ride across Victoria Harbour using the services of the iconic Star Ferry. It has been in operation since 1888 and the two-storey boat travels from the Star Ferry Pier in Tsim Sha Tsui to the Central and Wan Chai piers between 06.30 and 11.30 every day.

It is a charming way to cross the harbour but also a great option for some site-seeing. The oldest vessel in service dates back to the 1950s (look for a brass plaque on the central column for each boat's history). The upper deck (where first class is found) features wooden seating and both indoor and outdoor areas. Head to the equally charming lower deck for more space to walk around and good photo opportunities.

At each pier the designated Star Ferry attendants are dressed in navy sailors' uniforms and welcome in each boat. On one of the ferries – the *Shining Star* – harbour tours can be booked. Should the need arise, it is also possible to hire various ferries for private events.
Star Ferry Pier, Central Pier and Wan Chai Ferry Pier
+852 2367 7065
starferry.com.hk

⑦
Kai Tak Cruise Terminal, Kowloon
New horizons

More than a decade after the city's old Kai Tak Airport closed its gates, the repurposed site has been transformed by Foster + Partners into a gleaming silver cruise terminal. Built on the southern end of the old runway, the terminal boasts the largest rooftop garden in the city, which is open to the public. Amid the greenery, the garden features sweeping 360-degree views of the Hong Kong skyline along with sheltered spaces that are ideal for outdoor dining.
33 Shing Fung Road
+852 3465 6888
kaitakcruiseterminal.com.hk

Permission to land

Built in 1925, the old and iconic Kai Tak Airport ceased operations in 1998, when it was replaced by the current site at Chek Lap Kok. With a tight approach over densely populated Kowloon, no one who ever landed at the old airport has forgotten it.

Ship shape

The sculptural terminal was completed in 2013

Celebrity X Cruises

Sport and fitness
On the front foot

Hong Kong may be considered one of Asia's great concrete jungles but venture just a few minutes away from the main metropolis and you'll find hundreds of miles of accessible hiking trails and picturesque stretches of beaches for swimming and surfing. Parks and squares across the city house exercise equipment as well as everything from tranquil tai chi classes to strenuous cross-fit sessions.

Over the following pages we'll show you the best places to experience the lesser-visited side of Hong Kong. Take a hike with panoramic views over the skyline and a rewarding dip in the waves at the end. Alternatively, find respite from the heat with wakeboarding in a peaceful bay. While you'll also find some great hotel gyms and indoor pools here, we suggest you get outdoors to experience the best of Hong Kong. And once you're done, you can't go wrong getting pampered by one of the city's great barbers or masseuses.

Swimming
Strokes of genius

Dip your toes
Shek O's sheltered bay is great for a swim

(1)
Shek O Peninsula,
Hong Kong Island
Relaxed seaside village

For a prime yet convenient swimming spot head to Shek O, a small beach and fishing village at the end of a peninsula on Hong Kong Island's Southside. It is accessible by bus or a 20-minute cab ride from Central.

In a sheltered bay, it's a great place for a dip and you can rent parasols or deck chairs there for next to nothing. Grab lunch at Thai restaurants beside the car park; cold beers are available from bars towards the beach's East End. Otherwise, head to Black Sheep in the village for a pizza or delicious Mediterranean food at Cococabana's terrace on the beach.
Big Wave Bay Road

2
Tai Long Wan, Sai Kung
Idyllic scenery

Some might find it hard to believe that Tai Long Wan, or Big Wave Bay, is part of a large city like Hong Kong; its remote location makes it even more idyllic. To reach the bay on the Sai Kung Peninsula, in Sai Kung East Country Park, you can rent a sampan boat from Sai Kung town or hike for 90 minutes or so from the nearest road at Sai Wan Pavilion. Popular with surfers, the beach is also somewhere that you can camp out if you feel like it. A couple of small shacks serve food and surfboards can also be rented. During the summer it's a popular place for junk boats to moor.
Sai Kung East Country Park

3
Repulse Bay, Hong Kong Island
Resort-style convenience

One of the most exclusive areas to live in Hong Kong, Repulse Bay Beach has had a makeover thanks to the opening of the Pulse, a beachfront mall with bars and restaurants close to the promenade. The beach is a strong option for those who like their seaside time a little more developed.

Grab a drink at Limewood or a meal at Meen & Rice, which offers traditional Cantonese dishes. The beach is also equipped with showers and barbecue stands, plus a Chinese temple that you can explore. Think of this as the South China Sea's answer to Santa Monica.
Beach Road

Swimming pools

01 **Victoria Park swimming pool, Causeway Bay:** As well as being the oldest public swimming pool complex in Hong Kong, Victoria Park's indoor pool is also the city's largest. While many Hong Kongers lament the closing of the park's picturesque outdoor pool that shut up shop in 2013, the indoor space is extremely popular. It is home to an Olympic-size pool with adjustable depths and a 2,500-seat spectator stand.
lcsd.gov.hk

02 **Four Seasons, Central:** Only resident guests can enjoy the pool here but the terrace is one good reason to check in. While the 20-metre lap pool and cold plunge pool are worth a visit, it's the infinity-edge pool that seems to fall into Victoria Harbour that is the big draw. A café serves snacks to poolside sunbeds.
fourseasons.com/hongkong

Three more beaches

01 **Cheung Sha & Pui O, Lantau Island:** Take the ferry from Central Pier 6 to Mui Wo on Lantau and then jump in a cab (or bus number 1) to either Cheung Sha or Pui O beaches, two idyllic stretches of sand with great restaurants. On Cheung Sha we suggest The Stoep which serves South African and Mediterranean staples; Lantana does good pizzas. At Pui O head to Mavericks for either a drink or its beach-shack-style food.
South Lantau Road

02 **Lo So Shing, Lamma Island:** A popular place to live for Hong Kong's creative and freelance communities, Lamma is a 30-minute ferry ride from Central but feels a world away from the urban hubbub. With no cars permitted on the island it's a tranquil spot so we suggest visiting on a weekday when things are quiet. Head for the peaceful Lo So Shing Beach, just over an hour's walk from the ferry. While there are showers and lifeguards, you should pick up something to eat from Yung Shue Wan en route so that you can have a leisurely picnic.
Lamma Island Family Walk

03 **Tai Long Sai Wan beach, Sai Kung:** Small but perfectly formed, this white sandy beach is ideal for paddling in the break due to the gradual slope into the water. Savour the sight of spectacular mountain views as well as a couple of waterfalls and fresh water pools just up the hill behind the beach.
afcd.gov.hk

Cycling
City routes

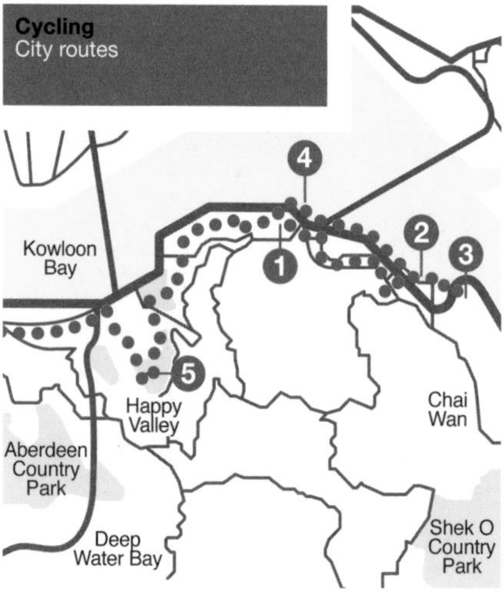

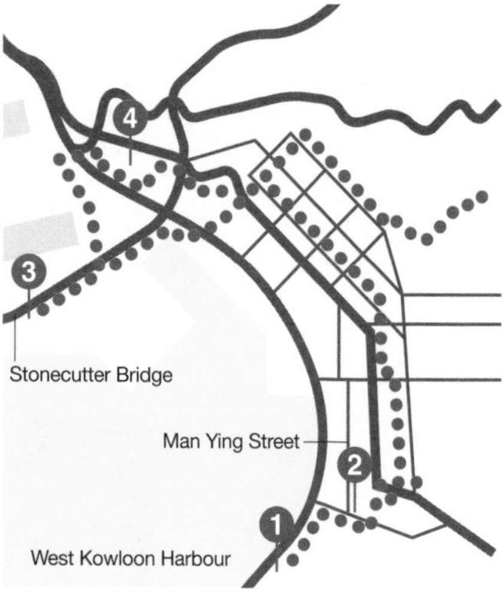

❶ Hong Kong Island
On the right track

DISTANCE: 17km
GRADIENT: Mostly flat
DIFFICULTY: Medium
HIGHLIGHTS: Shau Kei Wan old tram terminus; Hong Kong Stadium
BEST TIME: Evenings after 20.00 for lightest traffic
NEAREST MTR: Quarry Bay

This easily accessible cycling route traces the MTR's Island line and is a relaxing way to cover some highlights from Hong Kong's past. Beginning at ❶ *Healthy Street* in the North Point district, cycle east along Hoi Chak Street, cutting through Java Road playground. Continue onto Westlands and then Tai Koo Shing Road. Hang a left on Shau Kei Wan Road and another left on Tai On Street, which will lead you to the waterfront on ❷ *Oi Kan Road*. Cycle east until you hit the Island Eastern Corridor and then enter Shau Kei Wan Main Street East. Continue south until you arrive at the ❸ *old tram terminus*, built in 1904.

Cycle back towards the centre of the island. Next make a quick detour by turning right on to Lei King Road, looping around Tai Hong Street to pass by the ❹ *Sao Wan Ho Harbour Park* before resuming the route on Tai Koo Shing.

Upon reaching Java Road make a left turn instead of cycling straight back towards the starting point and continue along Tanner and King's Road, heading west towards Causeway Bay. At Tin Hau, turn left into Tung Lo Wan Road to arrive at the ❺ *Hong Kong Stadium*.

To get to Times Square and Russell Street you just need to cycle through Leighton Road and right on Matheson Street. Then it's a straight road west on Wan Chai Road and Johnston Road to end your cycle at Wan Chai MTR.

② Kowloon
Hidden gems

DISTANCE: 22km
GRADIENT: Mostly flat
DIFFICULTY: Medium
HIGHLIGHTS: Sea views from under Stonecutters Bridge; supper at Nam Shan estate
BEST TIME: From 18.00 onwards
NEAREST MTR: Kowloon

This cycling route takes you through some of the finer parts of old Hong Kong in Kowloon, weaving through the smaller and less congested side roads off the main thoroughfare, Nathan Road.

Starting at ❶ *West Kowloon Harbour* waterfront, head northeast and make a right turn on Jordan Road. Be careful while weaving through the busy streets and turn right on Ferry Street, before making a short detour at ❷ *Man Ying Street*.

Soak in the old street scenery as you cycle northwest, staying on the alleys and streets on the western side of Nathan Road.

Turn left at Hing Wah Street (just after Cheung Sha Wan MTR) and cycle all the way along Tsing Sha Highway until you arrive at the never-less-than-breathtaking ❸ *Stonecutters Bridge*, only accessible by bike and car. Take a moment to marvel and watch the sun set under the six-lane, 1.6km-long winner of the 2010 Supreme Award at the UK's Structural Awards. Then turn back and cycle along the same path, making a loop around ❹ *Lai Chi Kok*.

To round off the ride, cycle east towards Nan Shan estate at Shek Kip Mei MTR. At this point you will have covered nearly half of the district on the Kowloon Peninsula so reward yourself with some of the hearty, authentic cuisine that the area is renowned for before ending your ride at Kowloon Tong MTR.

Outdoor training
Fit for purpose

1

Tai chi, citywide
Inner calm

While Hong Kong can appear to have let many traditions go, the daily morning practice of tai chi is not one of them. Pass through even the most built-up of areas and you'll see groups of (normally elderly) Hong Kongers going through the fluid movements of the martial art.

While the groups in places such as Central's Statue Square or around Wan Chai's Harbour Road are unlikely to take you under their wing, masters Pandora and William will give you a lesson three mornings a week at a site behind the Cultural Centre that flanks Victoria Harbour. Head over for a 07.30 start on Monday, Wednesday and Friday. No booking is necessary. Teachers will be very happy to guide you through the exercises that form a core part of the beginning of many Chinese people's day.
Next to Serenade Chinese Restaurant
+852 9415 5678

This is how we justify breakfast

Hitting the heights

On the 11th floor of the Grand Hyatt in Wan Chai is one of the best hotel fitness set-ups; there is also a landscaped terrace with a large outdoor pool. It's all open from sunrise to sunset with views of the Central skyline.
hongkong.grand.hyatt.com

2

Surfing, Shek O
Total wipeout

Hong Kong is a great place to learn to surf. At Big Wave Bay you can rent surfboards, beginner foam longboards or easy body boards; windsurfing is also popular. While there are lifeguards on hand, don't paddle out too far if you're lacking enough experience: the waves can get pretty big in certain parts of the bay.
Big Wave Bay Road

3

Clearwater Bay Equestrian Centre, Sai Kung
Cowboy confidential

Many riding schools in Hong Kong are for members only but the Clearwater Bay Equestrian Centre offers lessons to non-members. Set in Clearwater Bay country park and situated on a peninsula, it offers various types of riding.
Lung Ha Wan Road
+852 6398 6241
ceec.hk

4

Wakeboarding, Tai Tam
Roll with the riptide

Head to the Wakeboard Centre in Tai Tam to spend a day speeding along behind a boat. The instructors there will guide you through everything from simple surfing to impressive tricks. During the heat of summer there is no better place to get some exercise.
101 Tai Tam Tuk Village
+852 9454 5772
wakeboard.com.hk

5

Coastal Fitness, Happy Valley
Horses for courses

There are various outdoor classes if you want a tough workout. One of the best places to head is the sportsground in the middle of Happy Valley racetrack. In addition to various courts and having pitches that are publicly accessible, it also has a good-size running track for a warm-up. Coastal Fitness organise classes on three mornings a week. Comprising running, TRX and kettleball exercises, these hour-long sessions aren't for the faint-hearted but are adaptable.
Happy Valley Recreation Ground, Sports Road
+852 2512 2262
coastalfitnesshk.com

Running routes
Kicking up the heels

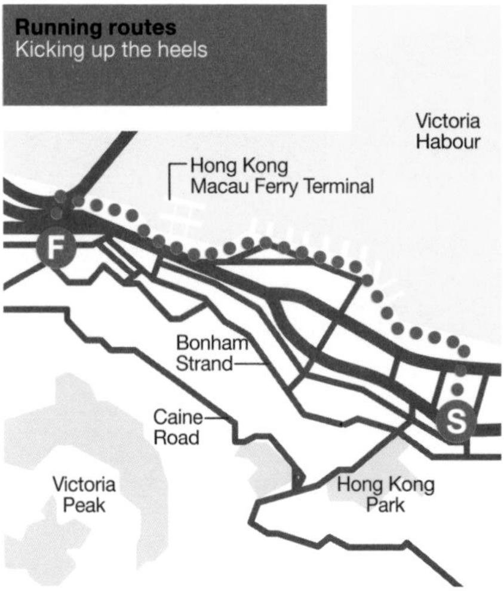

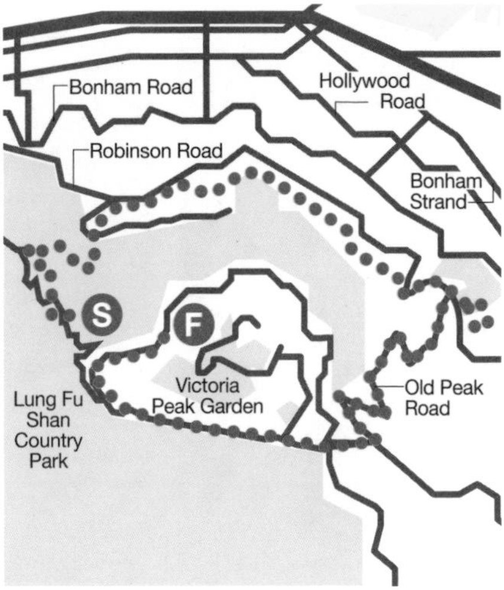

1
Central to Sai Ying Pun waterfront
Green scene

DISTANCE: 6km
GRADIENT: Flat
DIFFICULTY: Easy
HIGHLIGHT: Views across Hong Kong Harbour to the stunning Kowloon skyline as well as two small waterfront parks
BEST TIME: Weekdays to avoid the busy ferry piers over the weekend
NEAREST MTR: Admiralty

A quick and convenient run along the Victoria Harbour waterfront, this is a good route to take in some classic Hong Kong views without having to venture out of town. Start at the well-manicured Tamar Park, a rare patch of green in the middle of the city that is at the base of the Hong Kong Government's headquarters. Head towards the water and turn left onto the wide promenade running towards the soaring IFC tower. To your left you will see the austere building that is home to the Chinese People's Liberation Army Forces; to your right the harbour will open up. You will run past the Central ferry piers; first off are numbers 9 and 10 where junks and private boats dock, followed by the Star Ferry terminal and then piers taking people to the outer islands.

Once you have passed Ferry Pier 2, follow the path onto Man Kwong Street and run a short stretch along busy Connaught Road Central, past the Shun Tak Centre where the Macau Ferry leaves. Nip right through the Shun Tak car park and rejoin the waterfront promenade, following it all the way along until you reach the Sun Yat Sen Park. Here you can do a few loops around a lawn that has a statue of a Chinese revolutionary at its centre and make your way back along the same route to Central.

2
Morning Trail and the Peak
Rise and shine

DISTANCE: 9km
GRADIENT: Steep in parts
DIFFICULTY: Hard
HIGHLIGHT: Postcard-perfect views from the top of the Peak across Hong Kong and the Southside
BEST TIME: Weekday mornings before the hordes of tourists converge
NEAREST MTR: Central

This is a combination of a steep, uphill section ahead of a flat running route; you can always limber up by taking a brisk walk up the Morning Trail. Start out at the eastern end of Conduit Road and run along the undulating street, past some of the many residential towers for which the Mid-Levels are known. Follow this all the way along; just above Hong Kong University it becomes Hatton Road and veers to the left. This will take you directly onto the Morning Trail. Follow the signposts along the way that will take you up to the Peak.

At the top of the path there is a picnic area and small park on the right. Take a sharp left onto the historic Lugard Road, from where you will get panoramic views of Hong Kong. Follow this loop all the way around the Peak. Once you pass the busy tram terminus and Peak Galleria shops the road becomes Harlech Road, which has numerous fitness stations along the way for some pull-ups and stretches.

From here you will look out onto the island's Southside. Continuing in a circle, you'll get back onto Lugard Road. Follow this again and then just before you return to the Peak Galleria you'll see some steps to your left signposted for Old Peak Road. Pop down these and cool down on a tree-covered pedestrian descent that winds its way down to Hillsborough Court on Tregunter Path, where you catch a cab back into Central.

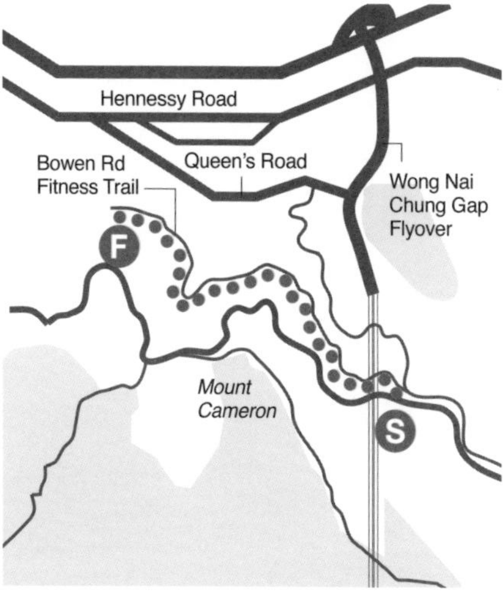

3

Bowen Road Fitness Trail

Simply shady

DISTANCE: 4km
GRADIENT: Minimal
DIFFICULTY: Easy
HIGHLIGHT: Getting a quiet, shaded taste of the city's underrated greenery while still in the shadows of the iconic skyline
BEST TIME: Weekday morning or dusk
NEAREST MTR: Central and Wan Chai

While only a few minutes' walk from Central, this pedestrian-only path is flat and shaded, offering convenient kilometre markers along the way. There is an abundance of stunning harbour views as well as the occasional snake to put a bounce in your step. This is a popular spot both for runners and those after a quiet stroll so be sure to stick to the right side of the path if you're just heading here for a walk.

Running from Central or Wan Chai to Bowen Road is a steep climb along twisting roads that, on one of Hong Kong's notoriously humid days, might end things before they start. Best to take a quick five to 10-minute taxi to the path's eastern entrance at Stubbs Road. From here, head west along the path. On a weekend there will be a good smattering of fellow joggers, dog walkers and tai chi practitioners.

At about 3km in you'll reach Wan Chai Gap Road to your left. Taking this turn will lead to a relatively easy two-hour hike to Wong Nai Chun Reservoir, where some of the fiercest fighting with the Japanese took place during the Battle of Hong Kong. Continuing on Bowen Road another kilometre leads to Bowen Road Park, where toilets and water are available. The path ends at Magazine Gap Road. Catch a taxi, walk 10 minutes downhill to Central or turn around and follow the path back.

4

Tai Tam country park

Run with a view

DISTANCE: 8km
GRADIENT: Undulating
DIFFICULTY: Intermediate
HIGHLIGHT: The views over peaceful reservoirs
BEST TIME: Morning or afternoon
NEAREST MTR: No stations nearby; taxis needed at start and finish

This run takes you along the banks of the Tai Tam reservoirs, built in the early 20th century to provide much of the island's fresh water. Start by taking a taxi to the imposing Hong Kong Parkview apartment complex. With your back to the apartments, turn right along Tai Tam Reservoir Road. This restricted access road is well shaded, so ideal for a leisurely run.

You'll pass the Tai Tam Management Centre on your left as the path turns right. Keep on the road. You'll round a bend and come downhill to two bridges; take the one to your left and continue on to the right, following signs to Tai Tam Road. Stick on this path. You'll cross another bridge and join Section 6 of the Hong Kong Trail. The path will descend and you will see a large dam through the trees and pass through a picnic area before getting to a stone bridge. Cross over and head straight on, along the edge of the reservoir and across various small bridges until you come down onto Tai Tam Road. From here you can grab a taxi back.

Where to buy

Kit yourself out for some trail running or swimming at Escapade (*escapade.com.hk*); spruce up your running gear at Nike Running (*nike.com*); and for surf gear head to Island Wake (*islandwake.com*).

Hikes
Best boot forward

To most visitors, Hong Kong is a city of speed and urgency. Streets are packed and busy, public transport is so efficient that A to B can pass you by in a blur and huge buildings seem to appear out of nowhere. But to Hong Kongers the city is also a place that offers nature on its doorstep. Getting out onto some of Hong Kong's hundreds of miles of public hiking trails, varying in length and difficulty, is one of the most popular ways to stay fit and healthy here.

If you are only in town for a couple of days there are plenty of trails to walk (or run) along on Hong Kong Island itself that can be accessed within minutes of leaving Central. If you have got more time to spare, head out to the New Territories or one of the outer islands to gain a different perspective on life in Hong Kong. Many of these hikes not only offer great views but also end up at one of the city's beaches, offering you a pleasant (and refreshing) reward for your toils.

You won't need a huge amount of specialist equipment for hiking in Hong Kong as paths are well kept, often paved and signposted. The only thing to watch out for is the pollution level, which can rise during winter. If it's high, head out to one of the hikes off Hong Kong Island. And make sure you are carrying water and sun protection as the biggest hurdle to hiking is the city's hot and humid weather.

Out and about
—
Hong Kong begs to be explored properly

1

Lantau Peak, Lantau Island
Top of the world

The second-highest peak in Hong Kong is the place to catch the sunrise over the city. There are various routes up to the peak and this hike takes around four hours. Start at Pak Kung Au, which has a relatively steep climb up some steps before things flatten out. The trail continues with steep ascents followed by short bursts of flat land. Right before you reach the peak you clamber up a stone "ladder" of high steps to the summit. Views onto Po Lin Monastery, the Big Buddha and miles of Hong Kong make it worth while. Head down the south side of the summit to reach the beach.
Tung Chung MTR

2

Dragon's Back, Hong Kong Island
Rollercoaster ride

One of Hong Kong's most striking nature trails, Dragon's Back is so called because of the resemblance of the hills' rolling ridges to the mythical creature's spine. Getting here is easy: from the Shau Kei Wan MTR, take the number 9 bus towards Shek O, alighting at the To Tei Wan bus stop. Alternatively, jump in a cab and let the driver know to drop you at the hike's starting point.

Taking between one and two hours, the trail takes you up an easy 284 metres to Shek O peak, from where you can see both Shek O and Tai Long Wan (Big Wave Bay) beaches. On a clear day, Tung Lung Island across the South China Sea will be just about visible in the distance. You will then trace the ridges of the D'Aguilar Peninsula before winding down to Tai Long Wan village, tucked behind the bay.
Shek O Country Park

3

MacLehose Trail Section 5, New Territories
Monkey magic

The 100km of the MacLehose Trail run offer some fantastic vistas. Section 5 offers a glimpse of Hong Kong history and views over Kowloon; there is also the likelihood you'll run into macaque monkeys. That said, keep your food packed away as these creatures are more aggressive than affectionate.

Allow between three and four hours for this hike. Walking the trail in reverse makes the start a little more accessible so we recommend beginning at Kowloon reservoir. You start with lots of flora and fauna, with signs along the way to describe it. There is also a colony of black kites at Eagle's Nest peak.

Continuing to Beacon Hill you will pass a couple of rest points in case you need a break. The tower on the hill is for aircraft navigation and you will pass pillboxes and other relics from the Second World War. At the Reunification Pavilion you can get great views over Kowloon as well as the old Kai Tak Airport. Then take the diversion to Lion Rock, an important landmark in Hong Kong's history. Following the path toward Sha Tin Pass, you can exit here and grab a bus back to town.
Tai Mo Shan Road

④
Wilson Trail Section 1, Hong Kong Island
Park and ride

The Wilson Trail consists of 78km of path that passes through eight of the city's country parks. It cuts across Hong Kong Island and over to the New Territories, with the only break being Victoria Harbour.

The first part of the trail is challenging and popular – often called the Twins thanks to a double hill between Wong Nai Chung Gap near Tai Tam and Stanley – and you can start at either end. If you're heading towards Stanley (and the beach) you'll begin at Parkview: an imposing red-brick development of residential towers built on the edge of Tai Tam nature park. The climb is long and steep at times but, towards the end, the view opens up and you can end your trip in the small market town with plenty of restaurants, market stalls and cafés.

Starting out at Stanley offers great views towards Violet Hill after a steep but contained climb. Once you arrive back at Parkview you can even continue onto the second part of the Wilson trail that will take you over to Quarry Bay. Or just jump in a cab home. Part one takes around two hours and is more challenging than Dragon's Back.
Hong Kong Parkview

Last time I travelled this far I was chasing a frisbee

Haircare and grooming

01 The Mandarin Barber, Central: For an old-school experience, this is the only place to go. The Mandarin Barber (*pictured*) on the second floor of the historic hotel has been in business since the 1960s. It offers the usual trims and shaves, and guests can also book facials or time with Mr So, the hotel's famous Shanghainese pedicurist.
mandarinoriental.com/hongkong

02 Hair House, Central: For a slightly more local experience, give Adam Chan a ring. Cutting the hair of some of Hong Kong's most fashionable men from a small space in Central, this two-man shop will give you the sort of short-back-and-sides that wouldn't be out of place in a 1950s diner. It's informal and friendly; if you're there after work you'll likely be offered a tipple from Chan's whisky selection.
+852 6255 5450

03 Emmanuel F, Central: Run by a French husband-and-wife team, this sleek salon specialising in organic and chemical-free products is perfect for a cut and blow dry – perhaps in its private VIP suite.
emmanuelf.com

Walks
— Find your own Hong Kong

Hong Kong's rich history has marked each of its neighbourhoods with their own unique spirit, be it a rough-around-the-edges industrial development or a traditional village smack bang in the middle of the city. Wherever you end up you'll find myriad restaurants and bars alongside parks and intriguing architecture. These four walks will guide you around our favourite parts so you can find your own preferred haunts.

NEIGHBOURHOOD 01

Kwun Tong
Restored and revitalised

While Kwun Tong may not be the most obvious destination for tourists, this neighbourhood on the eastern side of Kowloon Bay is in the throes of transformation. Yet if you know which nook to explore or corner to turn you will discover that the area is scattered with hidden gems, among them world-class art galleries, quality bike shops and well-designed civic spaces.

The staid office buildings are remnants of the post-Second World War period when the government earmarked Kwun Tong for redevelopment, drawing in thousands of labourers and entrepreneurs from the region and beyond to fuel Hong Kong's industrialisation. When it moved from a manufacturing to a services-based economy during the late 1980s, the factories emptied out. Fortunately, the introduction of the MTR at around the same time connected Kwun Tong to the rest of Hong Kong and brought in a new wave of tenants, among them scores of artisans and craftsmen drawn by cheap rents.

Today a pioneering spirit still drives much of the city's changes. In 2008 the government announced a revitalisation plan to spruce up the promenade and build more parks and gardens. The derelict façades of the industrial blocks belie the creative revival stirring within, making a day trip to Kwun Tong well worth it.

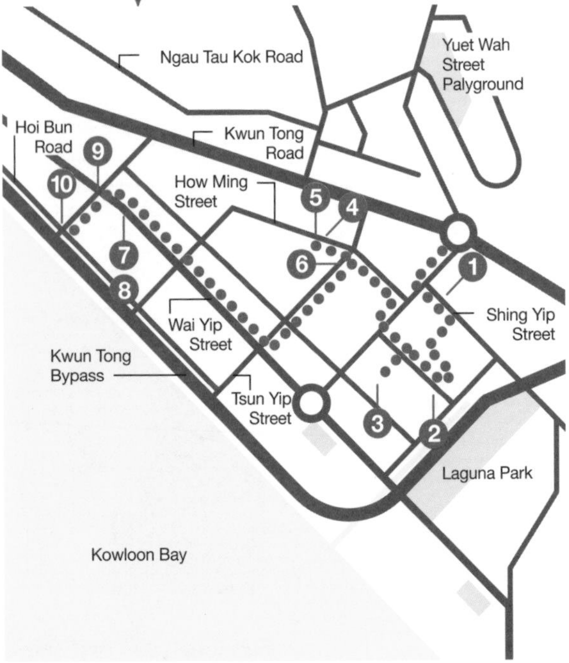

Gritty creativity
Kwun Tong walk

Don't let the grim, uninspired exteriors of Kwun Tong's industrial buildings fool you; this is where many Hong Kong creatives are settling and with them a number of quality cafés and independent retail options. From Kwun Tong MTR take Exit B1 and turn left on Shing Yip Street, starting your day with a cappuccino at 1 *Coffee Art*, a specialist in foam art. After your caffeine fix,

Getting there

Kwun Tong is easily accessible on the MTR. It spans Ngau Tau Kok and Kwun Tong stations on the green Kwun Tong line, which you can get onto at Yau Tong station from the West Rail line. The trip from Central takes about 30 minutes.

take a right onto a pedestrian-only alley at the Camel Paint Building and meander through souvenir stalls and snack stands, emerging at Hing Yip Street. Enter the parking garage of the Union Hing Yip Factory Building opposite and take the lift to the fourth-floor ❷ *Osage Gallery*, an expansive showroom that features some of the best emerging artistic talent from Hong Kong and beyond.

Cyclists should head to the adjacent building to stock up at Hughes Lau and Queenie Chu's ❸ *Bike the Moment*. Their cosy shop sells Tokyobikes along with everything an urban cyclist needs, from handmade leather saddlebags by Nothinglastsforever to Sögreni bicycle bells from Denmark. Leaving the building, wander northwest to the How Ming Factory Building, where you'll find vintage retailer ❹ *Growth Ring & Supply* on the fifth floor. After perusing the selection of antique furniture, homeware and knick-knacks from around the world, go down to the first floor for a hearty lunch at ❺ *Factory 99*, whose range of western dishes is a hit among locals.

To combat post-meal drowsiness, grab a coffee from ❻ *Caffé Essenza* next door at the base of Landmark East, the glassy twin office towers designed by US-based Arquitectonica, and enjoy it at the timber-decked Tsun Yip Street Playground. This civic space pays tribute to Kwun Tong's industrial heritage with an informative exhibition. After your history lesson, continue west towards the waterfront, turning right on Wai Yip Street. Saunter northwards where it's hard to miss the clean wooden front of the ❼ *Easy-Pack Industrial Building* that stands out from the rest of the dreary and dilapidated façades. Designer Aidan Li has converted this edifice into a hotbed of creative agencies, design studios and other innovative start-ups. If you have time to spare, consider taking a leather-making class at the ❽ *Butcher Lab*, conducted by the affable Momo Ngan.

What better way to end the day than with a stroll down the delightful ❾ *Kwun Tong Promenade*, which was once used to load and offload recycled paper? Now featuring a boardwalk, performing space and series of gardens, it's also the perfect vantage point to cast your eye across the water and behold the magnificent ❿ *Kai Tak Cruise Terminal* as the sun sets over the city. The UK's Foster + Partners was responsible for the boardwalk's eco-friendly design and its adjoining park warrants a visit in its own right.

Address book

01 Coffee Art
G46, E Plaza,
7 Shing Yip Street
+852 5403 7883

02 Osage Gallery
4F, Union Hing Yip Factory Building,
20 Hing Yip Street
+852 2793 4817
osagegallery.com

03 Bike the Moment
11F, Unit B11,
16-18 Hing Yip Street
+852 9823 9179
bikethemoment.com

04 Growth Ring & Supply
5F, Block AB, How Ming Factory Building,
99 How Ming Street
+852 3462 3288
gr-supply.com

05 Factory 99
1F, Room A, How Ming Factory Building,
99 How Ming Street
+852 2345 8333

06 Caffé Essenza
6F, One Landmark East,
100 How Ming Street
+852 2950 0130
caffeessenza.hk

07 Easy-Pack Industrial Building
140 Wai Yip Street

08 Butcher Lab
5B, Easy-Pack Industrial Building, 140 Wai Yip Street
+852 3421 0212
butcher-lab.com

09 Kwun Tong Promenade
178 Hoi Bun Road
+852 2341 4755
lcsd.gov.hk

10 Kai Tak Cruise Terminal
33 Shing Fung Road
+852 3465 6888
kaitakcruiseterminal.com.hk

NEIGHBOURHOOD 02

Tai Ping Shan

A slice of colonial past

Tucked away in the leafy backstreets between Sheung Wan's Hollywood Road and the residential Mid-Levels, the quiet neighbourhood that surrounds Tai Ping Shan and Po Hing Fong streets is home to many of Hong Kong's best independent shops, fast-food establishments and cafés.

Tai Ping Shan means "Peace Hill" and was once an alternative name for Victoria Peak. Under colonial Britain, Tai Ping Shan became one of Hong Kong's red-light districts following the relocation of many of the city's Chinese population from Central, which the British were redeveloping as the commercial district it is today. Tai Ping Shan was badly affected by the bubonic plague at the end of the 1800s, which led to it being cleaned up and the building of Blake Garden, as well as the establishment of the Bacteriological Institute in 1906, which stands today as an imposing red-brick building. You'll still see a few coffin-maker shops that made this their home as a result of the high number of the deaths in the area.

Thankfully, today Tai Ping Shan and its surrounding streets are far less grim. Having kept many of the old *tong lau* (shop houses) intact, modest businesses have been able to find spaces with street access. More walkable than many other parts of the city, it's the perfect place to while away an afternoon.

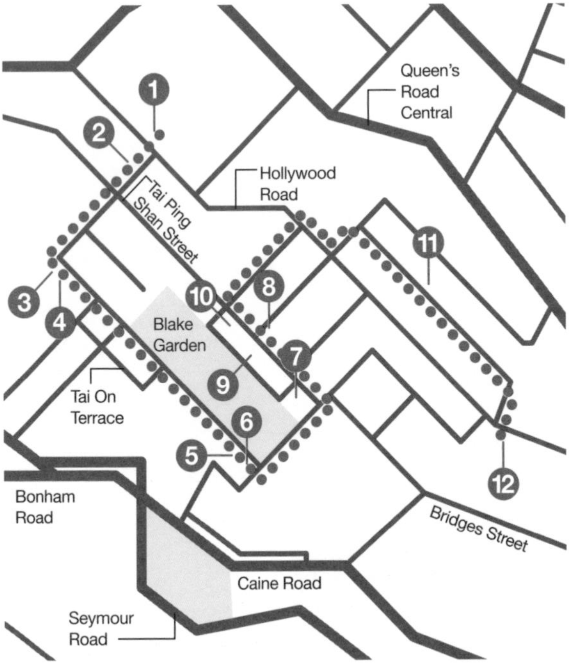

From temples to tea rooms
Tai Ping Shan walk

Start at the 1 *Hollywood Road Park*, which can be entered at the Queen's Road end of Hollywood through elaborate red Chinese-style gates. Inside you'll find ponds that are teeming with turtles. It's a popular place for elder members of the community to sit or do tai chi. The site is an important one as, before the construction of the park, it was called Possession Point and marked where the British Royal Navy landed (the shoreline used to be just down the hill from the park) before signing the Treaty of Nanking. This marked the end of the First Opium War and ceded the territory of Hong Kong to Britain.

Out of the park, cross back over Hollywood Road and grab coffee or breakfast at 2 *Corner Kitchen Café*, an airy two-floor space that sits on the corner of Po Yan Street. Make your way up Po Yan, where the first turning to your left leads to stairs up to Tai Ping Shan Street (we'll end up here later). Continue on the slight gradient until you reach Po Hing Fong Street, which is up another set of stairs to your left. Right on the corner here you will see 3 *Fungus Workshop*, a leatherworking studio run by two couples who offer classes and products that are for sale.

If you're in need of a manicure pop into 4 *The Nail Library* next door, which has made an impressive space out of an old building. Keep heading up the stairs and when the street flattens out you'll be on Pound Lane, the site of a much-contested new

escalator to connect the Mid-Levels to Sheung Wan. Go up the stairs here and do a little loop to see some of Hong Kong's old apartment blocks, complete with terrace planting and balconies.

From Tai On Terrace, head down the steps back onto Po Hing Fong Street, where you'll have a good view of the basketball courts in Blake Garden, a popular spot for spontaneous games. Take a right along Po Hing Fong; a number of small shops are set up along the quiet street. At the corner is 5 *Po's Atelier*, a sleek-looking bakery that offers goods from around the world and is a firm favourite. Tucked behind it is 6 *Café Deadend*, a great place to grab a sandwich; be sure to try to get a seat in the courtyard.

Head down the hill on Kui In Fong. If you feel like a rest, step into the Banyan-tree-shaded Blake Garden, a rare pocket of flora in the heart of the city. At the bottom of Kui In Fong, take a left onto Tai Ping Shan Street. You can't miss the bright orange awning of 7 *Yuk Kin Fast Food* on the corner of Old Kat Cheong Street, one of the only old-style cafés left and an extremely popular one. Walking down, pop into 8 *Amelie & Tulips* on the corner with Sai Street, a great two-floor space selling Scandinavian furniture and design. At number 18 is 9 *Juice*, a menswear shop run by Kevin Poon. And down the street at number 22, 10 *Mood* sells vintage workwear – a rarity in Hong Kong, where wearing second-hand clothes is somewhat frowned upon. There's also a small barbershop in the back.

At the corner of Upper Station Street, above Nosh café, is an old *tong lau* that has been restored into beautiful flats by Swedish designer Helen Lindman. Take a right here and a right again on Hollywood Road then a quick left onto Lok Ku Road where you'll see the 11 *Cat Street Market* off to your left on Upper Lascar Row. Here you can buy all sorts of memorabilia and trinkets.

At the end of the market take a right up the stairs and you'll end up opposite the 12 *Man Mo Temple*, a great place to finish under the myriad burning incense coils suspended from the ceiling.

Getting there

Tai Ping Shan is just above Sheung Wan Station on the MTR's blue Island line. If you're not in a rush, jump on a tram for a scenic view of the city. Get off at the Queen Street stop, walk up Queen Street and turn right onto Queen's Road.

Address book

01 **Hollywood Road Park**
Hollywood Road
+852 2673 3885

02 **Corner Kitchen Café**
226 Hollywood Road
+852 2547 8008
cornerkitchencafe.com

03 **Fungus Workshop**
4 Po Hing Fong
+852 2779 9003
fungusworkshop.net

04 **The Nail Library**
6 Po Hing Fong
+852 2803 2290
thenaillibrary.com

05 **Po's Atelier**
GF, 70 Po Hing Fong
+852 6056 8005
posatelier.com

06 **Café Deadend**
72 Po Hing Fong
+852 6716 7005
cafedeadend.com

07 **Yuk Kin Fast Food**
6A Tai Ping Shan Street
+852 2549 2505

08 **Amelie & Tulips**
GF, 56 Sai Street
+852 2291 0005
amelieandtulips.com

09 **Juice**
18A-B, Tai Ping Shan Street
+852 2517 3099
clot.com

10 **Mood**
22-24 Tai Ping Shan Street
+852 2559 8308

11 **Cat Street Market**
Upper Lascar Row
cat-street.hk

12 **Man Mo Temple**
124-126 Hollywood Road
+852 2540 0350
lcsd.gov.hk

NEIGHBOURHOOD 03

Star Street, Wan Chai

The best of old and new

Wan Chai is a busy and diverse neighbourhood on Hong Kong Island. Home to the noisy bars and clubs of the city's red-light district, it also hosts the offices of businesses big and small as well as government towers, new residential projects and charming old buildings.

The Star Street area is at the southwest end of the neighbourhood and is one of the best places to see historic and modern Hong Kong side by side. This cluster of streets was named after celestial objects in the late 19th-century following the construction of Hong Kong's first power plant here and the installation of a number of street lights. Demolished in the 1920s, the area saw its fair share of fighting during the Second World War. Today it is home to small and independent shops and cafés that offer a contrasting retail experience to the city's popular shopping malls. While many of the city's old, traditional shop houses (*tong laus*) have been torn down, those around Star Street have been preserved to retain their original function: small businesses occupy the ground floor and the upper levels are divided into apartments. Here, design studios, shops and galleries sit alongside modern Japanese restaurants, Hong Kong-style coffee shops and international fashion flagships.

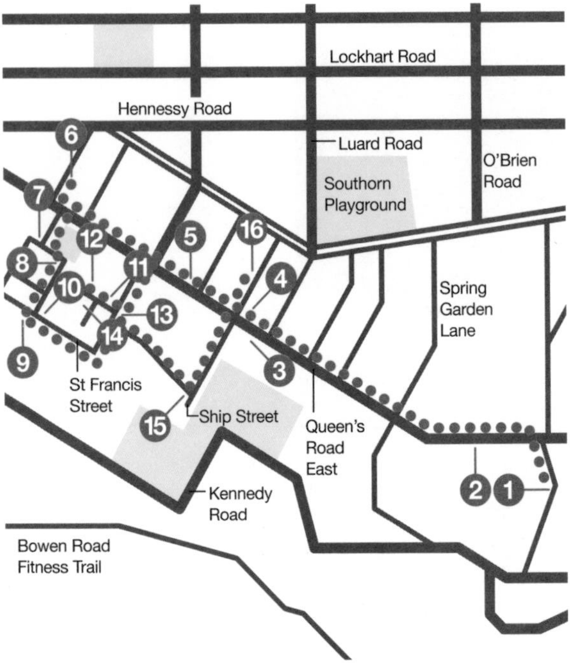

Sharp retail and traditional dining
Star Street walk

Occupied by a colourful mix of older apartment buildings and shiny new towers, this part of Wan Chai is a great insight into modern, busy Hong Kong.

Start your walk at Stone Nullah Lane and the ❶ *Blue House*, a bright four-storey building on the corner of King Sing Lane that has balconies running along its façade. Built in the 1920s, this rare type of *tong lau* was home to a famous kung-fu studio during the 1950s and today houses the Wan Chai Livelihood Museum and apartments. It's a rare example of a government-preserved historic tenement and is one of the city's architectural icons. Head back down Stone Nullah Lane onto

the bustling Queen's Road East and make a left. This road is lined with modern and traditional furniture shops, a wet market, offices and restaurants, and is a main thoroughfare for Wan Chai.

At number 221, on the corner with Wan Chai Gap Road, is the ❷ *Old Wan Chai Post Office*: the oldest surviving post-office building in Hong Kong. Built in 1912, it stopped taking mail in 1992 and now functions as an environmental resource centre, but the original red mailboxes are still visible inside.

Continue along Queen's Road East, passing the late 19th-century ❸ *Hung Shing Temple*. Crossing over Queen's Road to number 128 you'll find ❹ *King Tak Hong Porcelain* shop, a treasure trove of a store that sells nearly every

home furnishing imaginable and is a great place to pick up Chinese and Japanese porcelain. A little further along is ⑤ *Happy Cake Shop*, a well-known bakery and an unbeatable spot to grab breakfast or a snack.

Carry on along Queen's Road and turn right down Anton Street to grab a coffee at ⑥ *Coco Espresso*, the MONOCLE bureau's favourite coffee shop, before heading back across Queen's Road into Dominion Garden and up the stone steps at the back onto Sun Street. Here, pop into ⑦ *Kapok* to shop for emerging international brands (*see page 48*) and ⑧ *Eclectic Cool*, a well-stocked design shop. Follow Sun Street past the Mondrian-like waste disposal building and take a left into Star Street. Here you will pass the perfumerie ⑨ *Le Labo* and ⑩ *Olala Yat Wun Mien*: a charming noodle shop. Head into the small park and down to St Francis Yard, where ⑪ *The Monocle Shop* and bureau is located next to a selection of other great stores including women's clothing shop ⑫ *Vein*. There's also

Getting there

Centrally located, there are many way to get to the Star Street neighbourhood. The closest MTR stop is Admiralty. Take exit F for Pacific Place Mall. Just after you go down the escalators there's a sign posted on the walkway to the left that will take you to Star Street.

the much-loved ⑬ *Tak Yu cha chaan teng*, where tables of locals eating traditional rice and noodle dishes accompanied by Hong Kong-style milk tea spill out onto the street. It's our top pick for lunch in the neighbourhood.

Across the road from our shop you'll see a set of stairs heading up to ⑭ *Odd One Out Gallery*, where you can buy prints from around the world. If you continue along this street (which is called Sau Wa Fong) you'll find a number of great independent shops to explore (one of the best is unmarked; look for a blue-tiled exterior and tinted glass door) and well-planted green areas to rest.

The women's branch of ⑮ *Delstore* stocks some of Japan's best fashion brands. Ask here for directions to the men's shop as it can be a little tricky to find. From there (Schooner Street), turn left down the stairs of Ship Street, crossing over Queen's Road East again, and grab dinner at Jason Atherton's lively tapas bar ⑯ *22 Ships*. Then jump on the train at Wan Chai MTR Station.

Address book

01 **Blue House**
72-74A Stone Nullah Lane

02 **Old Wan Chai Post Office**
221 Queen's Road East

03 **Hung Shing Temple**
129-131 Queen's Road East

04 **King Tak Hong Porcelain**
128 Queen's Road East
+852 3118 2422
kingtakhong.com.hk

05 **Happy Cake Shop**
106 Queen's Road East
+852 2528 1391

06 **Coco Espresso**
GF, 2 Anton Street
+852 2529 1682
cocobarista.com

07 **Kapok**
3 Sun Street
+852 2520 0114
ka-pok.com

08 **Eclectic Cool**
5 Sun Street
+852 5699 6882
eclectic-cool.com

09 **Le Labo**
2F Star Street
+852 3568 6296
lelabofragrances.com

10 **Olala Yat Wun Mien**
2 Star Street
+852 2866 3381

11 **The Monocle Shop**
Shop 1, Bo Fung Mansion,
1-4 St Francis Yard
+852 2804 2323
monocle.com

12 **Vein**
2 St Francis Yard
+852 2804 1038
bvein.com

13 **Tak Yu**
2 Kwong Ming Street
+852 2528 0713

14 **Odd One Out Gallery**
14 St Francis Street
+852 2529 3955
oddoneout.hk

15 **Delstore**
3 Schooner Street
+2528 1770
delstore.co

16 **22 Ships**
GF, 22 Ship Street
+852 2555 0722
22ships.hk

NEIGHBOURHOOD 04

Tai Hang

Cosy harbourside haven

In the hustle and bustle of Causeway Bay it's hard to imagine that a small and quiet neighbourhood such as Tai Hang exists just minutes away. The village once sat directly on the harbour, with the original coastline running along what is now Tung Lo Wan Road. Tai Hang means "big water channel" and the area was a place where water would flow directly into Victoria Harbour through the valley where the harbour now sits at the base.

Today the reclaimed land that stretches into the harbour cuts Tai Hang off from the busy waterway and instead sets a park and sports ground between it and the shore. The small grid of streets at the heart of Tai Hang is the most interesting part of the neighbourhood. Every year the community mounts the now famous Fire Dragon parade. Groups of men practice for months ahead of the festival, perfecting their teams' dragon dances for when hundreds crowd Tai Hang's small streets to witness the procession of fire-breathing paper dragons accompanied by drums.

Most of the buildings here are converted shop houses. While some still house the garages and workshops that the area has been known for over the past decade or so, others have been transformed into cafés and restaurants, making Tai Hang one of the city's most popular places to dine.

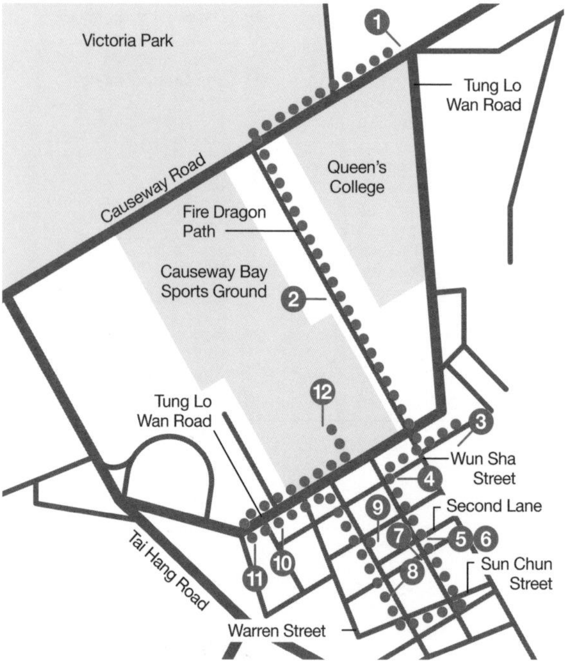

Village within the city
Tai Hang walk

Starting at ❶ *Tin Hau MTR Station*, take Exit B towards Victoria Park. Walk towards the playing courts along Causeway Road and pop into the green space for a walk around the track, a quick swim at the public pool or just to people-watch. Crossing over Causeway Road towards the tennis courts opposite the park, walk down the pedestrian-only ❷ *Fire Dragon Path*, a popular place for dog-walking and part of the route for the famous parade. Turn left at the top of the path and head to the ❸ *Lin Fa Temple*, just behind Tung Lo Wan Road on Lily Street. Originally built during the Qing dynasty, this picturesque temple is dedicated to Kwun Yam, the goddess of mercy; lines of worshippers regularly form to pay their respects.

Take a left up Ormsby Street where, on the corner with School Street, you'll see a beautifully kept Hong Kong home called the ❹ *Old School House*. Extensively planted and with its big windows often wide open, this place gives you a chance to take a little peek into a rare type of Hong Kong living. Continuing along Ormsby, get a coffee on the bench outside ❺ *Unar*, a neighbourhood favourite. It's a lovely spot to meet locals and watch the world go by. Above the coffee shop (and also housed in a well-restored shop house), the Unar team runs a homeware shop that is called ❻ *Feelsogood*. It sells a mixture of vintage furniture and industrially inspired light fixtures, with some smaller items for sale that make ideal gifts. Just across the street is 7 *Bing Kee*, a *dai pai dong* food stall serving traditional fare such as simple noodle soups that residents line up for every morning; join the queue for an authentic Hong Kong experience. It's run by a friendly man who will translate your order. There are many shops and cafés around this warren of streets so detours are recommended.

If you continue along Ormsby Street until you reach Sun Chun Street, take a right and walk past some of the old car workshops that are still in business and form the backbone of the neighbourhood. Make a right onto Brown Street where 8 *Go Ya Yakitori* is a popular spot for dinner and happy-hour drinks. At the corner of Brown and King Street you'll see a small hole-in-the-wall restaurant called 9 *Hong Kee* that serves up some of the city's best congee. If you're lucky you'll see the grandfather making fresh rice rolls.

When you're full, take a left at School Street and grab yourself a refreshing drink at 10 *Buddy Bar*, which you'll find on the corner of Jones Street, which fills with residents after work. A bit further down School Street is the deceptively named 11 *New York Club*, which is in fact famous for its Shanghainese meat balls and grew from being a small kitchen that served the car workshops. Making a right on Lai Yin Street, turn right again to walk back along Tung Lo Wan Road, past the 12 *Chinese Recreation Club* with its clubhouse and sports facilities as well as a coffee shop, bar and both a Chinese and western restaurant.

If you continue further up the road, crossing just after Fire Dragon Path, you will come to Wun Sha Street. Amble past the many restaurants and bars you'll find along the way until you see a playground on the right. Take the steps that head up the hill behind this onto Illumination Terrace and finally Tai Hang Road, where you can enjoy the view back to Tai Hang village. From here you can turn right along the leafy Tai Hang Road or take a cab back to Central.

Getting there

Tin Hau Station on the blue Island Line of the MTR is easy to get to. Otherwise both trams and buses serve Tai Hang well; get off these at Victoria Park. The number 10 bus goes all the way from Kennedy Town to North Point via Victoria Park and Tai Hang.

Address book

01 **Tin Hau MTR Station**
Causeway Road
mtr.com.hk

02 **Fire Dragon Path**
Causeway Bay

03 **Lin Fa Temple**
Lily Street

04 **Old School House**
4 School Street

05 **Unar**
4 Second Lane

06 **Feelsogood**
4 Second Lane
+852 2865 6168
feelsogoodls.com

07 **Bing Kee**
5 Shepard Street
+852 2577 3117

08 **Go Ya Yakitori**
21A Brown Street
+852 2504 2000

09 **Hong Kee**
11 King Street
+852 2808 4518

10 **Buddy Bar**
22 School Street
+852 2882 9780

11 **New York Club**
GF, 24 School Street
+852 6530 0288

12 **Chinese Recreation Club**
123 Tung Lo Wan Road
+852 2577 7376
crchk.org

Resources
— Inside knowledge

At first glance Hong Kong can seem complex and impenetrable; a confusing cluster of towering buildings connected above and below ground by walkways and home to thousands of businesses that are hidden away on their upper floors.

But in reality the city's chaos is organised. Governed by rules and good manners, easily navigable signs and an extensive public-transport network that is affordable, varied and efficient, Hong Kong is a pleasant and easy city to move around.

Hong Kongers are a welcoming bunch but knowing a few local terms, Cantonese words and popular songs will go far in impressing them. And with a subtropical climate that can switch from glorious sunshine to typhoon within minutes, you'll want to know the best places to enjoy both extremes.

Transport
Get around town

01 **Octopus card:** You can almost survive in Hong Kong without cash or credit cards if you have a topped-up Octopus. Used across all public transport, this handy card is also accepted in shops and cafés. Buy one at any MTR station for HK$150 (HK$100 value plus deposit). *octopus.com.hk*

02 **MTR:** Clean, efficient and well signposted, the MTR moves Hong Kongers around with ease. When exiting main stations such as Tsim Sha Tsui, Central or Causeway Bay, be sure to work out which exit you're after before leaving as walkways can stretch for hundreds of metres underground. *mtr.com.hk*

03 **Bus:** Hong Kong's double-decker buses are cheap and cover all corners of the city. There are also minibuses; those with red tops can stop and be hailed anywhere but green-tops have fixed routes.

04 **Tram:** These old streetcars rattle along between the east and west ends of Hong Kong Island. The system has been in place since 1904 and each ride costs just HK$2.30. *hktramways.com*

05 **Ferry:** From the Central Ferry Piers you can get to all of the city's outlying islands. For Lamma go to pier four and for Chueng Chau go to pier five. *starferry.com.hk*

06 **Taxi and private car hire:** Taxis are cheap and plentiful. You can hail them anywhere or wait at designated pick-up spots. The base fare is HK$22 for the first 2km. Each piece of luggage costs HK$5.

07 **Flights:** The Airport Express train will get you to Hong Kong International Airport in 24 minutes. Check in before getting on the train at Hong Kong or Kowloon stations. Taxis take around 40 minutes. *honkongairport.com*

Vocabulary
Local lingo

Cantonese is a fast-changing language. Here are some easy phrases to impress the locals.

01 **Beeh-tzao:** Beer
02 **Ciu Bao:** Very cool
03 **Ding ding:** Street trams
04 **Gei dor chihn ah?** How much is it?
05 **Ho Muhng:** Very cute
06 **Jo San:** Good morning
07 **Ng-goy:** Thank you
08 **Sap Sap Soy:** No big deal

Soundtrack to the city
Top tunes

01 **The Reynettes, 'Kowloon Hong Kong':** In the 1960s the economy was booming and Hong Kong was a land of opportunities. The tune not only reflects this optimism but also the pride felt in a world-class city.

02 **Ta-yu Lo, 'Queen's Road East':** The main artery of Queen's Road connects the financial heart of the city to relaxed, residential neighbourhoods. This song is dedicated to the road and the lives around it.

03 **Various artists, 'In the Mood for Love' film soundtrack:** If you romanticise the dim lighting and elegant silhouette of Maggie Cheung in her traditional *qipao* dress that set the scene for the film, this album will transport you.

04 **Beyond, 'Boundless Oceans, Vast Skies':** Made in the 1990s, this song's talk of dreams and freedom became the unofficial anthem for the Occupy movement in 2014 and was sung by thousands during protests.

05 **Blur, 'The Magic Whip' album:** While obviously not a local band, the Britpop darlings recorded their long-awaited eighth album in Hong Kong in the summer of 2013.

Best events
What to see

01 **Lunar New Year Fair, citywide:** Catch multiple events, including a night parade in Tsim Sha Tsui and big race day at Happy Valley.
January/February

02 **Hong Kong Marathon, citywide:** Popular despite the pollution, the best stretch to watch is the Central waterfront.
February; hkmarathon.com

03 **Art Basel Hong Kong, Hong Kong Convention and Exhibition Centre (HKCEC):** Work is shown from international and local galleries and artists.
March; artbasel.com

04 **Rugby Sevens, Hong Kong Stadium:** This condensed tournament is both a sporting spectacle and an excuse for a party.
March; hksevens.com

05 **International Film Festival, citywide:** Showcases talent from home and abroad at venues across Hong Kong.
April/May; hkiff.org.hk

06 **Cheung Chau Bun Festival, Cheung Chau:** The island's local community honours the god of fishermen with a colourful parade.
May; cheungchau.org

07 **Le French May, citywide:** This art festival represents France's huge expat population with food, films, performances and exhibitions.
May; frenchmay.com

08 **Stanley International Dragon Boat Championships, Stanley Beach:** This fun and noisy race is a great spectator sport.
June/July; dragonboat.org.hk

09 **Hong Kong Book Fair, HKCEC:** Book-lovers attend with suitcases to fill up with printed matter.
July; hkbookfair.hktdc.com

10 **Symphony Under the Stars, Happy Valley:** The racecourse is transformed into an outside concert venue for the Hong Kong Philharmonic.
November; hkphil.org

Rainy days
Weather-proof activities

Hong Kong's weather is rarely predictable. Sunny days during sticky summer months can be interrupted by typhoons and clear blue skies can soon cloud over. Times like this offer great excuses for exploring modern shopping malls and charismatic hotels.

01 **Shopping malls:** While we certainly don't suggest you do all your retail therapy in these temples to air-conditioning and international brands, they are great places to escape the changing climates. Many can be accessed direct from the MTR or via covered walkway, protecting you from the elements. Here are a few:

IFC Mall, Central: Sen-ryo Sushi, Lane Crawford and the Apple Store.
ifc.com.hk
Pacific Place, Admiralty: Good cinema and bookshop.
pacificplace.com.hk
Landmark, Central: Head to the basement for some of the best men's shopping in the city.
landmark.hk

02 **Hotel lobbies:** Historically these were places where the expat population would head for western food and entertainment. Today, often with preserved interiors and impeccable service, some are still worth a visit. At the Peninsula in Kowloon, the grand lobby serves a highly coveted afternoon tea, often accompanied by a live band. If you're in Central, head to the Mandarin Oriental where the Captain's Bar is the perfect place to while away the hours with a martini; at night there's usually live music. And in Admiralty, another spot where you can enjoy a drink accompanied by live jazz is the Lobster Bar and Grill at the Island Shangi-La, which (perhaps unsurprisingly) specialises in seafood.

Sunny days
The great outdoors

When the sun's out in Hong Kong, things can get very hot. Here are some good ways to cool off while still outdoors.

01 **Lamma Island:** Just 40 minutes away from Central is a quiet island home to much of Hong Kong's bohemian and creative community, where motor-powered vehicles are banned. City-dwellers head out here to escape with fresh seafood and cooler air. Two ferries serve the main villages of Yung Shue Wan and Sok Kwu Wan. Once you get there, explore the village restaurants and markets or make your way onto the paved Lamma Island Family Trail for a peaceful stroll. Try to avoid weekends, which can get very busy.

02 **Junk boats:** Forget the ones filled with inebriated expats dressed as sailors; hiring your own junk boat for the day makes for one of the best ways to see the city and beat the heat. On modern luxury yachts to more charming older seacraft, take a trip to a remote beach or do dinner while cruising the nightly light show on Victoria Harbour. Give Island Junks a call, who can arrange catering from Maison Eric Kayser and even an onboard masseuse.
islandjunks.com.hk

03 **Outdoor swimming pools:** Ranging from beautifully landscaped to charmingly old fashioned, there are a number of great outdoor pools for those looking to exercise or kick back and get a tan. Here are two of the best:

Kennedy Town: New and well equipped with options nearby for a post-dip lunch.
Kowloon Park: Three outdoor pools, sunbeds and an artificial waterfall make this pool a popular spot.

About Monocle
—— Take a look around

In 2007, Monocle was launched as a monthly magazine briefing on global affairs, business, culture, design and much more. We believed there was a globally minded audience of readers that were hungry for opportunities and experiences beyond their national borders.

Today Monocle is a complete media brand with print, audio and online elements – not to mention our expanding network of shops and cafés. Besides our London HQ we have seven international bureaux in Hong Kong, Toronto, Istanbul, Singapore, Tokyo, Zürich and New York. We continue to grow and flourish and at our core is the simple belief that there will always be a place for a print brand that is committed to telling fresh stories and sending photographers on assignments. It's also a case of knowing that our success is all down to the readers, advertisers and collaborators who have supported us along the way.

London calling
—
Midori House is in Marylebone

1
Print
Committed to the page

MONOCLE is published 10 times a year. We have stayed loyal to our belief in quality print with two new seasonal publications: THE FORECAST, packed with key insights into the year ahead, and THE ESCAPIST, our summer travel-minded magazine. To sign up visit *monocle.com/subscribe*. Since 2013 we have also been publishing books in partnership with Gestalten.

2
Hong Kong bureau
Eye on Asia Pacific

MONOCLE is published 10 times a year along with two new special publications: THE FORECAST is packed with key insights into the year ahead and THE ESCAPIST is our summer travel-minded magazine. All are published out of our London HQ with the support of our international bureaux. Launched in 2010, our Hong Kong outpost is headed by James Chambers and runs an extensive network of writers, researchers and correspondents across Asia. The team are regulars on Monocle 24 (*see right*) and ensure a steady stream of guests can appear on our shows live from the Hong Kong studio.

3
Radio
Sound approach

Monocle 24 is our round-the-clock radio station and was launched in 2011. It delivers global news and shows covering foreign affairs, urbanism, business, culture, food and drink, design and print media. In Hong Kong you can listen to *The Globalist*, which is regularly co-hosted out of our Hong Kong bureau and features interviews with special guests across the entire Asia-Pacific region. Our eclectic playlist accompanies you day and night, assisted by live sessions that are hosted at our Midori House HQ in London. Visit *monocle.com* to listen live or download shows via our app, iTunes or SoundCloud.

Style spot
Visit our Wan Chai shop for all things Monocle

④
Online
Digital delivery

We also have a dynamic website: *monocle.com*. As well as being the place to hear Monocle 24 – or, if you are a subscriber, have access to all the stories ever run in the magazine – the site is where we present our films. Beautifully shot and edited by our in-house team, these documentary gems provide a fresh perspective on stories reflecting our editorial philosophy.

❺
Retail and cafés
Good taste

Via our shops in Hong Kong, Toronto, New York, Tokyo, London and Singapore we sell products that cater to our readers' tastes and are produced in collaboration with the brands that we believe in. We also have cafés in Tokyo and London serving tasty lunches and reviving coffee among other things – and we are set to expand this arm of our business.

Monocle
EDITOR IN CHIEF & CHAIRMAN
Tyler Brûlé
EDITOR
Andrew Tuck
BOOKS, SERIES EDITOR
Nelly Gocheva

The Monocle Travel Guide Series: Hong Kong
GUIDE EDITOR
Aisha Speirs
ASSOCIATE EDITOR
Jason Li

DESIGNER
Jay Yeo

PHOTO EDITORS
Lois Wright
Poppy Shibamoto

PRODUCTION
Jacqueline Deacon
Dan Poole

Writers
Alexandra A Seno
Aric Chen
Mark Cho
André Fu
Lynn Fung
Michael Leung
Janice Leung Hayes
Liv Lewitschnik
Jason Li
Kurt Lin
Alan Lo
Vivien Lu
Tristan McAllister
David Michon
Chiara Rimella
Aisha Speirs

Chief photographer
Lit Ma

Still life
David Sykes

Photographers
Carmen Chan
Ben Quinton
Kenneth Tsang

Illustrators
Satoshi Hashimoto
Tokuma
Masao Yamazaki

Research
Cindy Chan
Keane Knapp
Kurt Lin
Alia Massoud
Marie-Sophie Schwarzer
Jeremy Toh

Special thanks
Mikaela Aitken
Paul Fairclough
Jared Flint
Maria Hamer
Hughes Lau
Edward Lawrenson
Lola Oduba
Ben Olsen

We hope you have found the Monocle travel guide to Bangkok useful, inspiring and entertaining. There is plenty more to get your teeth into: our London, New York, Tokyo, Hong Kong and Madrid guides are on the shelves as we speak, with Miami and Istanbul joining them in the coming months.
Cities are fun. Let's explore.

01
London
The sights, sounds and style of the British capital.

02
New York
From the bright neon lights to the moody jazz clubs of the US's starring city.

03
Tokyo
Japan's capital in all its energetic, enigmatic glory.

04
Hong Kong
Get down to business in this vibrant city of depth and drama.

05
Madrid
A captivating city that is abuzz with spirit and adventure.

06
Bangkok
Stimulate your senses with a mix of the exotic and eclectic.

07
Istanbul
Where Asia and Europe meet – with astonishing results.

08
Miami
We unpack the Magic City's box of tricks.